SYMBIOSIS

SYMBIOSIS

Writing and an Academic Culture

Kim J. Kipling
Richard J. Murphy, Jr.

Foreword by Anne Ruggles Gere

Boynton/Cook
HEINEMANN
Portsmouth, NH

BOYNTON/COOK PUBLISHERS
A Subsidiary of
HEINEMANN EDUCATIONAL BOOKS, INC.
361 Hanover Street, Portsmouth, NH 03801-3959
Offices and agents throughout the world

Library of Congress Cataloging in Publication Data

Kipling, Kim.
   Symbiosis : writing and an academic culture / Kim Kipling and
Richard Murphy.
      p. cm.
   ISBN 0-86709-313-7
   1. English language—Rhetoric—Study and teaching—Virginia—
Radford. 2. Interdisciplinary approach in education. 3. Learning
and scholarship—Authorship. 4. Writing centers—Administration.
5. College teachers as authors. 6. Radford College. I. Murphy,
Richard John. 1945–   . II. Title.
PE1405.U5K56 1992
808′.042′0711755786—dc20   92-28900
                                                                 CIP

Printed in the United States of America.
92 93 94 95 96 9 8 7 6 5 4 3 2

Contents

Foreword
by Anne Ruggles Gere
vii

Preface
Writing About Writing and Culture
ix

One
A Teaching Mission
1

Two
Beginnings
From Idea to Institution
12

Three
Writing Across the Curriculum at Radford
22

Four
Moments of Collaboration and Insight
32

Five
Faculty Writing and Learning
46

Six
Students Writing and Learning
62

Seven
Making a Community, Making a University
76

Eight
Creating an Image, Creating a Culture
88

Nine
Politics
Power and Persons
100

Ten
Academic Culture and the Spirit of Change
115

Foreword

This book enables us to *see* the writing-across-the-curriculum program at Radford University. As the authors note, "The professional literature on writing across the curriculum has tended to make seeing difficult [because] . . . in attempting to generalize, it has tended to schematize programs, reducing them to statements of ideas or lists of features that easily become clichéd in their abstraction" (116). Like Joseph Conrad who, in his preface to the *Nigger of the Narcissus,* asserts: "My task which I am trying to achieve is, by the power of the written word to make you hear, to make you feel—it is, before all, to make you see," Kipling and Murphy snatch moments from "the remorseless rush of time" (Dell, 1960, 27). They make us hear and see colleagues such as biologist Chuck Kugler, literary scholar Moira Baker, and musician George Parish along with events such as the president's annual convocation address and the faculty retreat at Pipestem State Park.

Even though we know a good deal about writing across the curriculum—effective approaches to use in classrooms, ways to foster collaboration among colleagues, the kinds of results we can expect from students—we know little about whole programs. The existing literature does not enable us to see and hear the development of writing across the curriculum from incipient idea to institutionalized program, nor does it allow us to see the same program from the multiple perspectives of those who participate in it as students, faculty, and administrators. This book does both. Although the authors played major roles in developing and maintaining the writing-across-the-curriculum program at Radford University, this is not their story; it is the story of a program and the institution with which that program has grown.

Unlike Conrad, Kipling and Murphy do not call upon the rescued fragment to reveal "all the truth of life" (29), but they summon various fragments to represent multiple "truths." They recognize what John Clifford, in his introduction to *Writing Culture,* calls the "partiality of cultural and historical truths" (Berkeley: U of California P, 1986, 6). Kipling and Murphy enact the partiality of truths about academic culture by continually shifting their angle of vision. We move from President Dedmon's 1990 proclamations about the contributions to student learning made by Radford's writing-across-the-curriculum program to Richard Murphy and Warren Self's 1981 colloquy with colleagues interested in incorporating more writing in their courses to an examination of the 1992 WAC program, a "gossamer thing, a program of 'opportunities,' of dynamic moments of collaboration and insight" (31) to failures and successes, the perspectives of individual instructors and the experiences of individual students, and an exploration of the relationship between the program and the institution of which it is a part.

No one of these angles of vision represents the entirety of writing across the curriculum at Radford. Taken together they create a sense of movements, forms, and personalities that helped shape events during a particular moment in history. Kipling and Murphy enable their readers to hear many stories through multiple voices; they create an interplay of expressions through artfully written accounts. These authors do not presume to offer a model for others to emulate nor do they suggest ways of institutionalizing writing across the curriculum. They simply attempt to render "moments" at Radford.

For all of its charm and capacity to dislodge the ground from which representations are made, this book does make an argument. It asserts the complex and organic interactions of programs and universities, and it characterizes these interactions as a particular kind of symbiosis. Eschewing the symbiosis of parasitism (such as fleas on a dog) or commensalism (such as remora on sea turtles), this book argues that the writing-across-the-curriculum program exists in a symbiosis of mutualism, where each party benefits the other equally, as do the sea anemone and clown fish or bees and flowers. The authors marshall considerable evidence to show the mutualism of writing across the curriculum and Radford University. In so doing, they offer new perspectives on both writing and universities, and we, the readers, become beneficiaries.

Anne Ruggles Gere

Preface

Writing About Writing and Culture

In Search of Excellence by Thomas Peters and Robert Waterman begins with an observation about the limits of representation: "the picture of the thing is not the thing" (New York: Warner Books, 1982, 3). Their particular reference is to Rene Magritte's series of surrealist paintings in which the sharply drawn image of a tobacco pipe is accompanied by the inscription "Ceci n'est pas une pipe" ("This is not a pipe"). Peters and Waterman are making a point about business. The hierarchical flow chart of a business is not the business. "Much more," they say, "goes into the process of keeping a large organization vital and responsive than the policy statements, new strategies, plans, budgets, and organization charts can possibly depict" (3). Peters and Waterman might also have gone on to make the same point about their book: the descriptions they provide are always partial; the subjects they portray always elude full representation.

This is an apt caution with which to begin our description of the Writing Across the Curriculum program at Radford University. Much more has gone into this program than is represented by its organizational chart, its budget, or a sketch of its history. It has been this "more," in fact, that we have tried particularly to highlight and explain. Like all academic programs, this one is conducted by real persons at work in real time in the context of an institution with a highly individualized character and culture. This dynamic and personal interaction is itself an essential part of the program's story. But though we describe that interaction in considerable detail—with narratives of particular moments and voices of particular individuals—

our account still necessarily misrepresents. With Magritte we want to say: this is not the program; this is not the university.

Nevertheless, we have been influenced in our decision to provide a detailed description by the "portraits" of six secondary schools in Sara Lawrence Lightfoot's *The Good High School.* Lightfoot explains that in her portraits she was seeking "to capture the culture of these schools, their essential features, their generic character, the values that define their curricular goals and structures, and their individual styles and rituals"—and, more than these—"the connections between individual and institution—how the inhabitants create the school's culture and how they are shaped by it; how individual personality and style influence the collective character of the school" (New York: Basic Books, 1983, 6). Such an approach was needed, according to Lightfoot, to balance more abstract and theoretical discussions of secondary schooling. What was needed was vivid description of the daily experience of people who actually inhabit the schools. Thus, telling stories "from the inside out," as she says, she rendered "individual faces and voices . . . in order to tell a broader story about the institutional culture" (7). Only by undertaking such a vivid portrait of the academic culture of Radford University do we think that the reality of its Writing Across the Curriculum program can be made legible.

The objectivity which Lightfoot as an outsider was able to bring to her portraits is impossible for us. Not only have we both been teaching at Radford for many years; we have both been intimately involved in the development and work of the Writing Across the Curriculum program here. One of us, Richard Murphy, was instrumental in beginning the program and was one of its faculty coordinators for seven years. The other, Kim Kipling, participated in a Writing Across the Curriculum workshop during his first semester and ever since has worked actively for the program—as a presenter at faculty panel discussions, as newsletter editor, and as a member of the faculty advisory council. We must admit our bias, then, at the start: we believe that this writing-across-the-curriculum program has been very valuable to Radford University as a whole, and that it has provided many students and faculty here with a deeply educative experience.

But our purpose is not to recommend it or to suggest that other institutions should regard it as a "model" to emulate. If anything, we want to argue the opposite. By subjecting Radford's program to close scrutiny, we want to suggest that its organization and character, its development and guiding ideas have been dependent on the particular context in which it has grown. Its life has been organic, not formulaic, and it has grown in an environment that nourished (and was nourished by) it in particular and unrepeatable ways.

To our knowledge, this is the only extended description of a college writing-across-the-curriculum program in print. The need for such a description has been clear for some time. Schematic outlines of different "programs" or lists of common organizational "features" of writing across the curriculum have blurred the very thing they have tried to convey: the way ideas about writing and learning which had been developed in the late 1960s and early 1970s in England were transplanted to the United States and institutionalized in some colleges and universities here. The process of "institutionalization" is very complex. When ideas and institutions meet, both change. The decontextualized descriptions of writing across the curriculum available to date have tended to abstract and homogenize it and thus to neglect, if not to deny, the dynamic process of change.

This description of the encounter between the ideas of writing across the curriculum and one institution is a story of personality and politics, of felt need and satisfaction, of adaptation and luck. As particular as our account is, it suggests a broader truth: that academic change is less a bureaucratic than a cultural phenomenon. Academic change is not a matter of importing ideas or structures whole from outside the institution, nor of imposing them. Academic change can not be expected to be swift. Ideas need time to evolve, even in the minds of persons who think they understand them, and to become familiar, particularly to persons who are suspicious or afraid of them. Structures likewise need time to grow in response to the demands of the situation, and they need to be flexible enough to harmonize with the institution within which they are to do their work.

In drawing and redrawing this portrait of Writing Across the Curriculum at Radford, we have come to see more clearly the culture of the institution within which we work and the complex processes of institutional change. We have come, too, to understand more fully the political nature of our own writing. The act of representing is never innocent, never without effects. Certainly the authors of *In Search of Excellence* understood this fact. Peters and Waterman were not only describing the workings of successful American companies, they were contributing to a transformation of corporate culture. Sara Lawrence Lightfoot also understood the power of portraiture. In the afterword of *The Good High School,* she explicitly discusses the impact of her portraits on particular individuals and institutions, and she refers more generally to the ways such writing may shape practice and promote organizational change. "Portraits," concludes Lightfoot, "are not static documents . . . . They directly touch the actors in the portrait and may speak more broadly to a diverse range of people concerned about the issues and ideas expressed in the piece" (378). Our portrait, too, is in important ways political; it is intended to have effects both within and beyond the institution. We hope that this description will advance change within the institution by further embedding certain ideas about writing and learning into its cultural fabric, and we hope this story will contribute to the broader discourse on academic culture and academic reform.

In telling this story, we have encountered a paradoxical stylistic problem: we have been unable to use the pronoun "we." Though we have tried to reflect the experience of many people over a number of years, ours is not a consensus account. We have been unable to speak *for* others or *for* the program, to say, "We thought this," or "We decided that." We have referred to everyone, therefore, including ourselves in the third person. This usage sounds artificial to us, but the experience of shared work and thought in the history of this program has been so fluid as to make "we," in this case, an inherently ambiguous word.

The documentary sources we have used in compiling this story include program proposals to the Radford University Foundation, the university administration, and the Commonwealth of Virginia; back issues of the Writing Across the Curriculum newsletter, *Writing & Learning;* annual reports submitted by the program coordinators to the university president; back issues of the university alumni magazine, *Radford,* and the faculty/staff newsletter, *Campus Currents;* copies of the president's convocation speeches; publications of faculty writing from weekend workshops and from writing-intensive courses; informal faculty and student evaluations of workshops and writing-intensive courses; archive records in the public information office; and informal notes we kept during our years of active work for the program.

We have also interviewed various members of the faculty, staff, and administration, as well as students, soliciting their memory, interpretation, and assessment of the program's development and significance. We thank them for their help and for the voices they have added to this portrait. In addition, we have solicited the reactions of a number of faculty to early drafts of this book. We have sought their help in detecting factual errors, misrepresentations, inaccuracies of tone, and omissions. We appreciate their willingness to read and discuss the manuscript with us and, in doing so, to examine again the shape, direction, and implications of the program.

Many other persons have had a shaping influence on Radford's program as well. Ann Berthoff, James Britton, Toby Fulwiler, Dixie Goswami, Mary K. Healy, Ken Macrorie, Nancy Martin, Lee Odell,

Denny Wolfe, and Art Young all have visited Radford as program consultants. In lectures and workshops which they have conducted here during the last ten years, they have helped Radford faculty in myriad ways to think and talk with one another about writing and learning. Their influence will be made explicit in the following pages, but we want to acknowledge at the start the crucial role they have played in the development of the Writing Across the Curriculum program at Radford.

Warren Self, now associate vice-president for Academic Enrichment at Radford, has been an enormous help over many years, not only in developing the program, but in shaping its ideas and the ideas of this book. It is no longer possible for us to trace the play of his thinking in our thought, but we know that his insight into both the program and the university have time and again clarified for us the story we were trying to tell.

Not only has the program been valuable to us each individually; it has brought us together in an intense personal collaboration. For two years, we have talked and written together about this program. We have challenged each other, remembered differently, tested our interpretations on one another. We have spent hours walking along the magnolia avenues on Moffett Quad with Nancy Martin, explaining our story to her and listening to her advice. We have become regulars at the Deli Mart over on Jefferson Street, where, with the groundskeeping crews on their breaks, we have repaired for coffee and talk about our own teaching. For, all the while we have been working on this book about writing and learning, we have been teaching. As has always happened for us in this program, the three are inseparable.

When Noel Eggleston, late professor of history, read that last sentence, he penciled an encouraging "good" in the margin. Eggleston was one of the earliest faculty participants in the Writing Across the Curriculum program at Radford. For nearly a decade, he lent his sober, thoughtful voice to its faculty dialogue about writing and learning. His commitment to teaching and his respect for colleagues and students were essential to the program's development and an inspiration to all of us who worked with him. In the midst of what would turn out to be his last illness, he generously read and critiqued a late draft of this book. We want to dedicate it to him, therefore, in gratitude both for his ideas and for his incomparable example.

Chapter One

A Teaching Mission

Thirty-four brick buildings on a plateau of wide lawns, spearheaded by the tallest building between Roanoke and Tennessee, Radford University is a conspicuous presence in this small town. Norwood, Radford's main street, is State Highway 11, once the principal north-south thoroughfare in southwestern Virginia. Now, since Interstate 81 opened and took away its truck traffic, it is little more than a country road, meandering from town to town. For just a couple of miles, the New River on its way from North Carolina to Ohio bends in to run along Norwood Street. Between the river and the street are the Norfolk and Western railroad tracks. For many years, Radford's students came to school by train. A sandwich shop across from the university campus displays enlargements of grainy old black and white photographs: young women in long dresses with parasols and square leather valises, arriving at the train station for another school year.

Established in 1910 as the State Normal and Industrial School for Women, what is now Radford University became Radford State Teachers College in 1924. It offered its first baccalaureate degree in 1935, was renamed Radford College in 1944, became coeducational in 1972, and changed its name again, in 1979, to Radford University. At its beginning, and for much of its history, Radford was a school whose academic purpose was to train teachers. Teaching was its entire business. Informal estimates credit it with preparing 80 percent of all the teachers in the public schools in southwestern Virginia between 1910 and 1970. But during the last two decades, teacher training has become no longer its sole function as it has expanded and diversified its programs and worked to write for itself a new charter. Growing, changing, Radford University is in the process of defining itself as a comprehensive academic institution.

Twenty years ago, fewer than four thousand students enrolled at Radford College; now the university enrolls nine thousand, half again as many as the permanent population of the town. The last weekend in August, the students arrive—to banners strung by downtown merchants across Norwood Street and fluorescent signs in the windows of Kroger and Food Lion: "Welcome Back." Their return means the end of summer doldrums, renewed business at the video stores, expanded church congregations. It means sorority car washes on Saturdays in nearby Fairlawn, additional Meals-on-Wheels volunteers, and red and blue plastic cups scattered on lawns and in gutters the mornings after weekend parties. Their arrival is ambiguous: color and congestion, energy and noise, litter and laughter. Like college students everywhere, Radford's undergraduates seem to some observers fresh and hopeful, eager to learn and grow. To others, they seem lazy and amoral, confused by ennui and purposelessness.

These are the college students of America. If Radford University's statistics are not quite the national average, its student profile is very typical. The university enrolls more women (63 percent) than the national average, but most Radford students (93 percent) are white, and most are young. The median age of Radford's undergraduates is 20. The mean SAT scores of new freshmen are 445 verbal and 470 quantitative. Most Radford students work part-time during their undergraduate years. The students want to major in business fields in greater numbers than in any other academic discipline. Between 1984 and 1989, the number of graduating business majors has exceeded the combined total of the next eight most popular majors. Though they are attending school in the rural mountains of Appalachia, most Radford students are either *from* urban centers in Virginia or neighboring states or are headed *to* urban centers to pursue careers. And a still large proportion of them are the children of parents who did not attend college themselves. In some cases they are the first persons in their families to enroll in any postsecondary school. The last weekend in August, neighbors walk their young children and dogs along Tyler Avenue to watch the laborious unloading as new freshmen arrive and upperclass students move back into their dormitories and apartments.

None come by train any longer. Now, pickup trucks, station wagons, compact cars with rented plastic storage bins strapped on the roofs, U-hauls, and vans crawl along Tyler and Adams and Norwood Streets, looking for places to park. Red plastic milk crates filled with clothes and laundry detergent, mattresses, lamp shades, electronic keyboards, fans, lacrosse sticks and skateboards—

sidewalks are piled with stuff waiting to be carried up the dormitory stairs and down the hall. Commotion and laughter, shouted instructions, cicadas in the trees, the bolts of pre-drilled lofts being hammered with the butt-ends of wrenches, rap music blaring from a box carried by an orange-capped guy with a purple duffle bag, moving himself in, solo.

The weekend students arrive, the faculty convene, too, for department and college meetings and for a university-wide assembly in the main-stage theater of Porterfield Hall. They enter randomly through the many doors on either side of the theater, a few wearing business suits; many in shirt sleeves; some in sports jackets, sundresses, skirts; some in jeans. Many faculty are just returning from lunch where, after a morning of meetings and junk-mail, they talked house politics and summer school, NEH Summer Institutes, and too-short vacations to Myrtle Beach or California.

Four-fifths of Radford's approximately 500 faculty members are full-time; of those, more than half are tenured. Their average age is 46, though more than half of them are younger, and at least half have been teaching at Radford five years or less. Thirty-four percent of the full-time faculty are women.

The normal teaching assignment for Radford teachers is four three-hour undergraduate courses per semester or the equivalent in laboratory or clinical supervision. Most of the courses Radford faculty teach are called "general education" courses. They are often introductory, enrolling mostly students seeking to fulfill graduation requirements. Fewer of the courses Radford faculty teach are advanced or specialized, and fewer still are at the graduate level. Fourteen of Radford's thirty-five academic departments offer advanced programs leading to master's degrees or post-baccalaureate certification. None grants a doctorate.

Eighty percent of the faculty at Radford have themselves earned a doctorate or other terminal degree. The universities from which they come number a hundred, most in the United States, a few abroad. Most of Radford's teachers, therefore, were trained at institutions unlike the one in which they teach, and—there is only anecdotal evidence for this and inference—chose Radford *because* of this difference. Prospective faculty members visiting the campus see a number of signs that the primary institutional commitment of Radford University is to teaching and learning. The university mission statement, for instance, declares it: "First and foremost, the university emphasizes teaching and learning and the process of learning." The third page of the university catalog, after the table of contents and the academic calendar, lists "Faculty Award Recipients," highlighting some of those faculty who are "wholly committed to the institution's primary emphasis on teaching." In outlining the university's criteria for faculty evaluation, the *Faculty/Staff Handbook* lists three areas of performance: teaching, professional contributions, and university contributions. The evaluation procedures stipulate that no less than 60 percent of a faculty member's evaluation must depend on teaching.

In recent years, the university has seemed to some faculty to be attempting to increase the importance of "research" in its mission. A few departments have established publication targets for their faculty. Within the past two years a new center for brain research has been instituted at Radford. There is also talk of redistributing the percentages by which faculty work is weighted in evaluations. But at the same time, teaching assignments have continued to be demanding, the library has remained modest, and the general pattern of personnel decisions suggests that faculty promotion and tenure at Radford do not necessarily depend on substantial publication. All of these signs point to the kind of academic environment in which most faculty at Radford want to work, an environment in which the principal work they do—teaching—continues to be valued.

The nature of a so-called "comprehensive" university, however, tends to complicate any teaching mission it professes. According to the guidelines of the Carnegie Foundation for the Advancement of Teaching, comprehensive colleges and universities are classified by the levels of degrees they offer, the number of students they enroll, and the "comprehensiveness of their mission." Radford belongs to the category of institutions with enrollments of more than 2,500 that "offer baccalaureate programs and, with few exceptions, graduate education through the master's degree. More than half of their baccalaureate degrees are awarded in two or more occupational or professional disciplines such as engineering or business administration" (The Carnegie Foundation for the Advancement of Teaching, *The Condition of the Professoriate,* [Princeton, NJ: The Carnegie Foundation, 1989] 147–48). In reporting its activities, assessing its programs, applying for funding, and otherwise describing itself statistically, Radford compares itself to other institutions in this same category.

The special usefulness of this classification is in determining what Radford is *not.* It is neither a liberal arts college nor a research university. Unfortunately, the classification does not help to define very clearly what it *is.* Along with other schools so categorized, Radford is attempting to serve a variety of needs. Liberal arts, technical and professional training, undergraduate education, postgraduate certification—Radford's programs are a miscellany of offerings. In claiming a teaching mission for itself, therefore, Radford is in one sense being nostalgic. Such a claim seems to belong to another, simpler, moment in its history. The demands of comprehensiveness, of increased student enrollment, of professional education programs, and of the accrediting agencies that oversee them—all press against a genuine institutional commitment to teaching.

In *Scholarship Reconsidered,* Ernest Boyer has identified this as a common problem facing comprehensive academic institutions: because their functions are so various, their unifying purpose is especially difficult to define.

> Many of these institutions—offering a broad range of baccalaureate and master's level programs—are having a difficult time sorting out priorities. . . . What we urgently need are models for the comprehensive institutions, distinctive programs and priorities that give distinctiveness to the mission and are not purposely imitative of others. (Princeton, NJ: The Carnegie Foundation, 1990, 61–62)

In Radford's case, over the last twenty years institutional growth has required that it diversify its offerings and thus diminish its traditional role as a teacher-training college. But because its cultural identity for so long depended on its teacher-training function, growth has also required that it develop a new sense of itself, a new mission. The university is still in the process of shaping and articulating that mission, but already it is clear that at the center of its emerging definition of itself, it has placed "teaching."

Teaching is a timely theme. The news is full of calls for a renewed emphasis on undergraduate teaching in American colleges. Urged by the media, as well as by reports like those of the Carnegie Foundation, major research universities are anxious to declare that they have not relinquished their commitment to undergraduate students. Institutions like Radford, however, are voicing a similar commitment. Review their recruitment videos and alumni magazines. Without either large graduate programs or extensive research obligations, colleges like Radford are making concerted efforts to represent themselves as, first and foremost, teaching institutions. Such a claim may be little more than a cliché. To make good on it, a college must find ways to enact its words, to embody its aspiration in its daily work. The values implicit in a teaching mission—of study and creativity, of personal interaction among learners in a community of scholarship—must be so fostered by the institution as to become part of the academic culture itself.

One of the ways in which Radford University is attempting to define itself as an institution is illustrated by the speech that faculty convened to hear in August, 1990. Ordinarily, the president's annual convocation address is a state-of-the-university message, his one opportunity in the year to update faculty on budget and building, enrollments and planning. In 1990, however, quality teaching was the central focus.

The spring before, two Radford faculty had been publicly recognized for exemplary teaching—Grace Edwards, the chairperson of the Appalachian Studies Program, and Steven Pontius, then chairperson of the geography department, now Dean of the College of Arts and Sciences. Both had been selected by the Virginia State Council of Higher Education to receive Outstanding Faculty Awards, the first teachers from Radford to be so distinguished. The university president took the occasion of the convocation speech to honor them and to reflect publicly on their achievement.

Edwards, at Radford since 1980, is the director of the Highland Summer Conference and now also the chairperson of the English department. Along with her other work, she is currently developing a living history museum and is continuing her own research into the influence of Scottish culture on the early settlement of this region. Except for the computer table along one wall, Edwards's office looks like a combination museum and front parlor. Her bookcases are decorated with dulcimers and baskets, corn-husk dolls, and quilt patterns. On the floor next to her desk is a braided rug and a rocking chair. Business in this office is like a visit, and faculty and students who come here are made to feel as welcome as guests. That is one of the features of her teaching that former students admire and appreciate. She makes them feel important. She involves them personally in creative and scholarly projects. One student describes Edwards's teaching this way: "She shows [us] our roots, makes us proud of them, and 'calls' us to educate other generations as she does."

Pontius was recognized by the State Council for developing Radford's small geography department particularly in the direction of geography education. Together with his colleagues, he has worked to produce maps, atlases, and other materials for teaching geography. The Geography Alliance, an association of university and public school teachers in Virginia, is centered at Radford under Pontius's leadership. With support from the National Science Foundation, his department has built a sophisticated computer system for teaching students how to process and use geographic information. Like Edwards, Pontius is credited with a personal influence on students as well. Beyond the classroom, he works with them in a variety of ways—as a member of the faculty-student Judicial Board, as an advisor to a fraternity, as a faculty participant in the university's summer orientation program. He has the reputation for being both a demanding and approachable teacher. As in Edwards's case, too, Pontius's state-wide recognition followed his receiving one of the university's annual awards for distinguished teaching.

It was not unusual for the president to single out specific teachers for recognition during his convocation speech. It is one of the ways he works to validate the university's claim to be devoted to teaching. Almost every year, he pauses to acknowledge some particular person or project—Ed Hall, for his work in coordinating ideas and planning for Radford's Global College; Mike Cronin and George Grice, for developing a wider university emphasis on speech and establishing an oral communication program; Alex Weiss, for preparing and conducting a semester-long university program on the Holocaust experience and for bringing, among others, Elie Weisel to campus to address the university community.

Such notices of individual faculty are sometimes particularly personal. In the 1990 speech, for example, Myrl Jones was singled out, having just returned from a year of Fulbright teaching at the University of Kasel. Jones's German colleagues and students had been amazed by the time he had devoted to his work. For days they would watch him in his windowed office, conferring individually with students on drafts of their writing. "They saw what we've seen for years," the president said to the Radford faculty, "and they came to love him as we do."

But the message of the 1990 speech was general as well. "I am proud," the president said, "that Radford has an outstanding faculty committed to the learning process. You place teaching first and foremost among your priorities, and our students widely acclaim your willingness to help and to regard them as individuals."

Though addressed to the faculty, the annual convocation speech is not only for them. It is also for the public. Representatives of the local media are always present in force with cameras, tape recorders, and notebooks, and a copy of the president's remarks is distributed from the university's public information office, for release at 1:00 p.m., the moment the speech is scheduled to begin.

The public purpose of the speech helps to explain both its style and its refrain. The president's style is distinctive. A professor of communications and professional speech consultant, he reads with zest from a typescript in a binder resting on a lighted lectern. The lower right hand corners of the pages are often prefolded so that he can turn them easily and without halting. Sometimes he punctuates his phrasing with the flourish of a turning page, sometimes by removing his reading glasses and adding an extemporaneous (and usually joking) tangential remark. He alternately informs and amuses. He mocks himself as a powerless president. He expresses his pride in Radford in an ironic combination of hyperbole and understatement. He speaks one moment, for example, of Radford's national reputation, then in the next of its unpretentiousness:

"We get some things done because we don't know we can't. I rather like the dumb way of doing things." He typically looks for ways to connect himself to his audience's experience. "I'm a parent, too," he tells new parents at freshman orientation, and he says it with such comic weariness and exasperation that, in their laughter, they are sure he understands. In many different contexts, he reminds his listeners that he is a teacher. "My title reads Professor and President in that order. I like the first part better than the latter." When he undertook to examine teaching in his 1990 convocation speech, he drew his rhetorical premise from a sense of shared purpose with the faculty. "After all, all of us became professors because . . . we wanted to be teachers, and it's only natural that we should continue to explore what it is about the profession that drew us to it."

As for his refrain—the emphasis on teaching at Radford University—it recurs in presentations the president makes to audiences of parents and potential students during recruitment tours each spring. It is always part of his message to the university Board of Visitors, to the Virginia state legislature, to regional media in periodic interviews, to the readers of *Vital Speeches* (where his addresses are sometimes reprinted), to alumni, and to new students and their parents at the summer orientation sessions called appropriately "Quest."

This is a teaching institution, he says. The faculty is here to teach. They chose Radford because it was a college that would allow them to teach and reward them for it, and Radford chose them because they are individuals whose first professional priority is teaching. It is a burgeoning faculty, young, energetic, and committed to close personal attention to undergraduate students. Though it is not as small an institution as it was for many years, the president continues to stress the virtues of smallness for teaching. Radford faculty, he says to parents, are here to teach your children. He tells students to take advantage of the relatively small class size; you will be able to meet your professors, he says, and work closely with them.

If the 1990 convocation speech had a local focus (to recognize distinguished Radford University faculty) and a personal slant (he called the last section of it "Personal Reflections on the Nature of Teaching"), it also had a distinctly public purpose. Its title—"American Higher Education: The Restoration of Quality Teaching"—set it deliberately in the context of the public debate about college teaching in America.

Surveying a number of current reports critical of the teaching in American colleges, the president declared:

Clearly, there exists today a widespread belief that teaching should be restored to its place of central importance . . . it should become the focus of the entire system of higher education.

He went on to quote Donald Kennedy, then president of Stanford University, asserting that teaching should be restored as the university's "primary task." He pointed to Ernest Boyer's Carnegie Foundation report (already being publicized before its release) as calling for a redefinition of scholarship that would "further dignify undergraduate instruction." And he claimed that the most familiar dilemma in American higher education is that the college says teaching really matters, but then it grants raises, promotion, and tenure to faculty based on their research. "Many of our colleagues," the president concluded, "are fed up with such forked-tongue claims."

Against this background, he sketched an image of Radford University. "Frankly," he said, "the great national concern for the lack of emphasis on teaching is misplaced when it comes to Radford. We've had our priorities straight for some time. As a matter of fact, years ago Radford articulated a position on teaching and research which is precisely what the national critics are calling for today."

It is always a university's job, among other things, to articulate its mission for different constituencies. When a college is in the midst of a period of intense growth and change, as Radford University is, this task is particularly demanding. It is both the public outside and the members of the university community itself whose idea of the institution must be shaped and expressed. Radford's representation of itself, then, as illustrated by the president's account of it, can be seen to be part description, part aspiration. Not only does it characterize what is, but it projects what might be. "We must continue to dream dreams," the president has said, "to think the improbable, if not the impossible, for this institution and its students."

Some observers are skeptical of the image Radford projects of itself. They regard its self-assertions as duplicitous. They are unconvinced that Radford *is* as committed to teaching and learning as its public profile insists. Some faculty, for example, complain that heavy teaching loads, burgeoning class size, and an underdeveloped library make *good* teaching at Radford increasingly difficult. Some students regard the university's academic challenge as only modest; even more believe that the public at large views a Radford education as second- or third-rate. And—as if to validate that perception—they wear tee-shirts that say, "C'mon, Radford! Let's Party!" and "Radford University—the Best 5 or 6 Years of Your Life."

To some observers, the president's speeches seem more rhetoric than substance. Some are made uneasy by his characteristic intensifiers, "frankly" and "precisely," and they regard his claims about Radford's national reputation as inflated. They are distrustful of both his style and his motives. The president does not seem to mind. "They say I'm overzealous," he quips to audiences in an aside, then adds that he has no intention of changing. Many of a college president's constituencies, he jokes, "presume that the president's motives, by definition, must be ulterior." It is clear, in fact, that his critics are part of his intended audience. For at least one element in the public program Radford University has undertaken for itself during his presidency is to change their minds about the place.

In the twenty years since Donald Dedmon became Radford's fourth president, both enrollment and the size of the faculty have more than doubled. Its dormitory rooms have become packed; it can now accommodate only a third of its undergraduate students in on-campus housing. Three new office, classroom, and student-activity buildings have been constructed. The athletic programs have been admitted to Division I of the NCAA. The graduate college has been expanded, and three academic chairs have been endowed. The growth story of Radford, however, is more than a story of numbers. It is a story of radical change. The Radford College of pre-1972 is so different from the Radford University of 1990 that what has been happening in the interim might fairly be called the invention of a university.

Such a project may be advanced by many different means: innovative ideas, good press, resourceful administration and faculty, well-maintained buildings and grounds, strongly accredited academic programs, and a vigorous social and cultural life. But these different facets require integration. They need to seem coherent if the "university" is going to seem whole.

In emphasizing teaching, Dedmon seems to be trying to provide one such integrating purpose. The first step toward reform in higher education, he said when he first came to Radford, is for the academic community to reexamine its own purpose, and this self-examination must be accompanied by renewed commitment. "The academic community," he continued, "will have to reaffirm its commitment to and support of effective teaching." So the recognition of Edwards and Pontius in his 1990 convocation speech was not only part of his theme, but another enactment of it. The speech—and the reception in their honor following it; the first such reception in Radford's history on behalf of the achievement of individual faculty—were designed themselves to reaffirm the university's commitment to teaching.

What does it mean to teach well? Dedmon asked.

First, it means that teaching and learning are inseparable. The teacher cannot be "teaching" if no one is "learning." It is not the teacher's job to go through the motions of lecturing, explaining, illustrating, and testing, as if these were acts whose ends were achieved automatically. It is not true, Dedmon declared, that what is taught is what is learned. Indeed, "even if it were the case that what we teach is precisely what our students learn, such 'teaching' makes little sense in any environment other than a *static* one. Our world—the world of our time—is not static; it is in flux." So our principal preoccupation as teachers ought to be the "facilitation" of student learning.

Second, the classroom in which this facilitation is most likely to take place is one in which faculty and students alike are learners. "When students and professors *both* aspire to learn," Dedmon said, the conditions are right—"something happens synergistically"—to make the classroom a genuine learning environment. Students work actively and responsibly; faculty are fair, open, and available, prizing both individual ideas and personal worth. In their meeting of purpose, in the personal relationship between the teacher and the student, true learning can take place.

Third, faculty should be striving, beyond the specific purposes of their own disciplines, to help students become independent learners. How we think and feel, understand and change, as we grow as individuals in a changing world—this, Dedmon asserted, should be the emphasis of higher education. Far more important than the product is the process by which we learn, and it is this which good teaching aims particularly to foster and understand.

In this August convocation speech, Radford faculty heard the president restate—but in a more sustained way than ever before—the university's commitment to quality teaching. By way of evidence of that commitment and the aspiration implicit in it, he pointed to the accomplishments of particular teachers on the faculty. Then he went on to cite again an example which has grown familiar to his Radford audiences: the Writing Across the Curriculum program. Every year since it was established by faculty in 1982, Dedmon has mentioned and applauded this interdisciplinary program. Its purpose—to help faculty and students focus, through writing, on teaching and learning—has converged with the university's purpose—to represent itself as an academically serious and integrated institution. The story of this program's development, therefore, is inseparable from the story of the institution in which it has taken shape.

Teaching and learning? Dedmon asked, rhetorically. That's what we're committed to here. "That's why we have the Writing Across the Curriculum program."

Chapter Two

Beginnings
From Idea to Institution

Nancy Martin recalls that, in the summer of 1968, she and her fellow teachers in the London Association for the Teaching of English (LATE) prepared a brief statement about language in the primary and secondary schools of Britain. In part, the statement—what they sometimes referred to as their "manifesto" in those tumultuous times—suggested that schools encourage more talk among pupils. "Children talking in small groups," the statement claimed, "are taking a more active part in all their work. Tentative and inexplicit talk in small groups is the bridge from partial understanding to confident, meaningful statement" (quoted in Martin, "Language Across the Curriculum: Where It Began and What It Promises," *Writing, Teaching, and Learning in the Disciplines,* ed. Anne Herrington and Charles Moran [New York: Modern Language Association, 1992] 15).

As modest a statement as that now sounds, Martin remembers that it was the product of intense intellectual excitement. For several years, these teachers had been reading current psychological explanations of language acquisition. They had been talking with each other and formulating questions to guide their observations of pupils in their schools. With the newly widespread availability of tape recorders, they had been recording student talk, analyzing its features, and meeting to discuss their findings. The word "manifesto" suggests how radical a view toward learning they felt themselves taking.

Their concern with talk paralleled the simultaneous concern of researchers at the London University Institute of Education with the development of writing abilities among secondary students. Martin was a member of both LATE and the Institute faculty. Together, the two groups found themselves investigating different facets of the role of language in learning. As soon as they undertook their first small-scale studies of talk and writing in school, they realized that they could not confine their investigation to English classes. "All the language encounters of the school day," Martin writes about that early discovery, "had become our field of study, thus, although it was as yet unnamed, 'language in the curriculum' had become our focus" (14).

The writing-across-the-curriculum movement in American colleges and schools during the last two decades has grown out of those late-sixties summer meetings of LATE. Martin and her colleagues decided to issue a book that would "stress, to scholars and the general public, the importance of talk in learning in all subjects" (Martin, 15). She credits the book, *Language, the Learner and the School* (1969) by Douglas Barnes, James Britton, and Harold Rosen, with being "the launch of Language Across the Curriculum" (15). It was followed rapidly by several other publications—James Britton's *Language and Learning* (1970), Britton's *The Development of Writing Abilities 11–18* (1975), Martin's *Writing and Learning Across the Curriculum 11–16* (1976), and the Bullock Report, *A Language for Life* (1976). Together, these books constituted what Martin calls "the beginnings of a research literature concerned with both spoken and written language across the curriculum" (16), and their ideas soon spread not only through the United Kingdom but also abroad.

One of the ways by which they made their way into colleges and universities in the United States was through the influence of the National Writing Project. Certainly, this is how they came to Radford University.

In 1977, Richard Murphy—one of the co-founders of the Writing Across the Curriculum program at Radford—completed a doctorate in English at Berkeley and became a teaching-consultant with the Bay Area Writing Project. He found teachers in the project taking it for granted that improving student writing would require the cooperation of teachers outside English and language arts classes. Project teachers were talking excitedly about *Language and Learning.* The Bullock Report was being read. Mary K. Healy, an elementary school teacher and one of the co-directors of the project, just back from studying with Britton and Martin in England, made a summer presentation to project fellows about the ways informal talk could help students learn. In the next two years, Healy organized a number of cross-curricular inservice programs for local school districts. She asked Murphy to help her and others in the planning of one of these programs. They sat together on the floor of her Berkeley apartment and sketched out a year-long series of workshops for the district's teachers. As it turned out, Murphy did not actually participate in carrying out this program, but he brought its orientation with him when, in 1979, he moved to Radford to take a teaching position in the English department.

In that same year, Warren Self, already on the English faculty at Radford, completed a doctorate in English education and became co-director of the Southwest Virginia Writing Project. That position brought him into contact with the directors of other writing project sites in Virginia and into their discussions about possible writing across the curriculum programs in their respective colleges. Four public colleges had already received funding from the State Council of Higher Education (SCHEV)—Virginia Tech, George Mason, Virginia Commonwealth, and Virginia State. Discussions were underway for expanding the number of participating colleges, and a loose, informal consortium was formed. When Murphy arrived in Radford, Self invited him to join these exploratory discussions.

Neither of them had any clear plan for Radford. With their common experience of the Writing Project's summer institutes for teachers, however, they vaguely imagined arranging some sort of summer institute for Radford faculty. But there was no money for such an institute and no immediate prospect of any, and the longer they attended the consortium meetings the clearer it became that the Commonwealth of Virginia would probably *not* expand the program it was funding at the four pilot institutions.

For two years, 1980–1982, Self and Murphy traveled to the consortium meetings—driving up and down the state to the University of Virginia in Charlottesville, to Richmond, to George Mason University outside Washington—and met and talked with other participants. Among these were some very informed and helpful individuals—Chris Thaiss from George Mason (then the convener of the informal group, now the director of the National Network of Writing Across the Curriculum Programs); Denny Wolfe from Old Dominion University (since the co-editor of a collection of essays on writing across the curriculum); C. W. Griffin from Virginia Commonwealth (since the editor of *Writing and Learning Across the Disciplines* and author of "Programs for Writing Across the Curriculum: A Report").

The discussions were exploratory and generative, but neither Self nor Murphy can remember any mention of Nancy Martin or her colleagues in London or their ideas about the heuristic power of language. There was excited talk about the book Elaine Maimon and four of her colleagues at Beaver College had just put out, *Writing in the Arts and Sciences* (1981). But the consortium agenda was mostly of politics and structure and funding and—assuming a program could in fact *be* instituted—how to get faculty to consider using and teaching writing in courses outside the English department.

Murphy and Self came no closer to any explicit idea about what they might do at Radford. Mostly, they spent the two years developing their own collaborative relationship and talking for hours on the road about other things: their experiences with Writing Projects in Berkeley and Virginia; their work in the Virginia Association of Teachers of English; and their teaching together in the English department at Radford.

Despite their shared interests and common experiences, Self and Murphy were, in many respects, an odd couple. A native Virginian, Self had graduated from Virginia Military Institute with a bachelor's degree and an army commission in 1965. While on active reserve, he earned a master's from the University of Virginia. For two years, from 1967 to 1969, Self was on active military duty, first as an artillery training officer at Fort Sill in Oklahoma, then as a personnel and civic affairs officer in Vietnam. By mail from Vietnam he applied for a teaching position at Radford and, in the fall of 1969, was hired as a temporary instructor of English. While teaching full-time, Self earned a doctorate in English education at neighboring Virginia Tech.

Before coming to Radford in 1979, Richard Murphy had never been east of Lake Tahoe. Raised in Oakland, California, Murphy attended college at the University of Santa Clara, then graduate school at Berkeley. In 1968, as Self was headed to Vietnam, Murphy was applying for conscientious-objector status. He dropped out of graduate school, married, taught high school for two years, then returned to Berkeley to complete his doctorate, specializing in eighteenth-century British literature.

Different in background, Self and Murphy differed in personal style as well. "There's an image that Warren and Rich worked well together," Self remarked at a recent Writing Across the Curriculum workshop, "like a pair of horses perfectly in harmony, pulling a plow with a single goal and purpose always perfectly shared." In fact, he confided, they are "less like two peas in a pod than like scrappy siblings—yin and yang." In manner, Warren Self is reserved, courteous, diplomatic. In his work, he is intuitive and decisive, more often guided by hunch than by plan. Richard Murphy, on the other hand, is outgoing, solicitous. He exudes enthusiasm but thinks and works with cautious deliberation.

On the interstates of Virginia, Self and Murphy became friends. Eating ice cream cones, wandering through the University of Virginia bookstore between meetings, talking about school and children and Vietnam, they helped each other form ideas about writing and learning. Without a program of their own or any immediate prospect of one, they were watching, listening, and assessing what little they knew of the programs of others. Their criticisms were impressionistic, based largely on intuition, but as they formulated them, their own ideas took shape.

They knew very early that they did *not* want to set up a program in which faculty from the English department would serve as consultants to faculty from other departments, advising them on how to construct and evaluate writing assignments. They had no objection to faculty working together. But they could not imagine how to *structure* such collaboration without making it seem that the consultants knew how to do something the other faculty did not. Later, at different times and for different reasons, they would develop graver doubts about such a program. They would come to question the assumption that the "something" called "writing" was fixed and consistent across courses and disciplines; that faculty from the department of English actually had expertise that other faculty lacked; that creating and evaluating writing "assignments" should be the focus of attention; even that writing itself should be the primary concern. But at the time, their reservations were simpler. They supposed that they *could* be helpful to other faculty, but offering to help seemed presumptuous to them, and neither Self nor Murphy could imagine how to frame it with enough diplomacy to have it taken seriously.

They did *not* want to create a program like the one they saw reflected in *Writing in the Arts and Sciences.* Self and Murphy did not actually know very much about the work being done at Beaver College. But based on their impressions of the textbook, they knew they wanted to do something different. *Writing in the Arts and Sciences* did not look like writing across the curriculum. It looked like a freshman English program; in fact it declared itself to be such: "The book is designed for use in the English composition course, since it is there—or nowhere—that undergraduates can learn to see themselves as academic writers and readers" (Cambrige, MA: Winthrop, 1981, xii). That phrase—"or nowhere"—ran directly against Self and Murphy's intuition. "Everywhere else," they wanted to counter. Writing across the curriculum, they imagined, ought to be structured to permit students to learn to see themselves as academic writers in many other courses and departments. They have since learned much more about the Beaver College program, and the history of writing across the curriculum in the United States will credit that program with a large and valuable influence. But for Murphy and Self, it served largely as a catalyst for thinking that they wanted something else.

The something else was not a junior-level competency exam in writing or undergraduate tutors or companion courses designed to add a writing component to courses in other disciplines or required writing courses in departments outside English. All of these seemed tangential to the emphasis both Murphy and Self thought a writing-across-the-curriculum program at Radford should have. Influenced by the common sense claim they had heard in the National Writing Project, Murphy and Self thought students would learn to write better if they wrote in all their courses. This meant something very different from imposing an exit-exam on students before they could graduate. And it meant that students should write in *all* their courses, not just in specially designed "writing" courses.

Murphy and Self also thought—but they did not make very clear to themselves why—that the *teachers* in these other courses should be responsible for the writing assignments. They felt that to bring in tutors to confer with students on drafts and to evaluate student writing was somehow to miss the point. In their judgment, the companion course structure suffered from the same defect. Both of these kinds of programs seemed to be saying, implicitly, in their very structure, that writing is not essential enough to this course for the instructor himself or herself to make time for it. Murphy and Self later read a structural critique of writing across the curriculum in American colleges by Cy Knoblauch and Lil Brannon, "Writing as Learning through the Curriculum" (1983). It articulated their shared sense that, whatever form it took, the program they would like to see in place at Radford University should not be English Across the Curriculum.

This sketch of the beginnings of Radford's program is deliberately a personal history. It emphasizes purposely the desultory progress of thinking by two individuals from a single institution. Now, more than ten years later, the large outlines of the writing-across-the-curriculum movement are much clearer than they were then. The phrase itself— "writing across the curriculum"—has become so familiar as to be a cliché, and a misleading one at that, since it refers to so many different things. But even the differences have by now become clearer. In the early eighties, for Self and Murphy and their colleagues in the Virginia consortium, writing across the curriculum was new and indefinite and rich with possibilities.

For both Murphy and Self, the most appealing possibility was to provide for their colleagues something of their own experience in the National Writing Project. Without having ever named it as such, they had already participated in a cross-curricular language program. They had already been introduced to a model for bringing teachers together from different disciplines, backgrounds, grade-levels, and interests. Poets and mathematicians, literary critics and historians, high school teachers, kindergarten teachers, principals and professors—Murphy and Self had already worked with such mixed groups. They had themselves felt the excitement.

In the summer institutes in Berkeley and Blacksburg, they had themselves experienced the benefit of listening to fellow teachers talk about their teaching. They had joined small writing groups (though both had doctorates, it was the first time either of them had participated in a writing group). They had written drafts and brought them to their peers for comment and criticism, and they had seen their finished writing collected in photocopied booklets and distributed to all the contributors. They had been expected to make formal presentations to their colleagues, identifying problems or solutions in the teaching of writing, drawing on illustrative samples of student writing, devising instructive activities for their fellow teachers, and fielding their questions and comments. They had experienced the way the institutes always left time for breaks and food—so that talk about teaching could go on spontaneously and informally in a social atmosphere. It was an extraordinary model of collaborative work and learning. Its success in the United States and abroad is by now well known. But in 1980, when Self and Murphy were beginning to imagine a writing-across-the-curriculum program at Radford, their felt experience of the National Writing Project informed all their thinking.

In March of 1981, Murphy and Self, together with an English department colleague, Susan Kirby, convened a meeting for Radford faculty. As Kirby remembers it, the meeting was called partly in response to inquiries by various faculty from the history and biology departments. Concerned about the quality of their students' writing on essay exams, these teachers had approached Kirby for advice. With deep roots at Radford (Kirby's mother had graduated from Radford State Teachers College in 1929; she herself was a 1966 alumna and had been on the faculty since 1967) Kirby was well-known on campus for her expertise as a teacher of composition. And in 1980, while Warren Self was co-director of the Southwest Virginia Writing Project, Kirby had participated in the Project's summer institute in Blacksburg. Like Self and Murphy, she was strongly influenced by the experience of working with teachers from diverse disciplines in a supportive, collaborative atmosphere. "I came out of that experience," Kirby recalls, "a practicing writer." She also came away with new ideas about the teaching of writing. Approached by concerned teachers, the three Writing Project veterans invited faculty to come together to talk about writing. The meeting—they called it a "colloquy"—was scheduled for a weeknight, in the small classroom on the fourth floor of Young Hall designated as the Writing Center. They didn't know if anyone would come.

But in fact the room was crowded. More than twenty-five teachers attended, some sitting at desks, some around tables, some standing. Murphy, Self, and Kirby talked—too long, they thought afterwards. But they made time for discussion, and faculty voiced some concerns about their students' writing and some uncertainty about whether they could or even should be trying to teach writing themselves. One participant, biologist Chuck Kugler, hazarded the tentative opinion—he put it more as a question than a statement—that the teaching of writing ought to be the responsibility of all teachers. Shouldn't it? Then the meeting adjourned for cookies and coffee and informal talk. Some of those present agreed to meet together in small writing groups. Self had suggested in his talk that they might try such a thing. And when the question was raised whether another meeting should be held, there seemed to be enough interest to justify it. So a second colloquy was planned for two weeks later. With this small start, and no clear sense of where it would lead, Radford's faculty had begun to think about writing across the curriculum.

It was not what Murphy and Self had been imagining. They didn't think it was possible simply to announce a meeting and have people show up. They had no idea what faculty would say in the event that they *did* come. They didn't even know what they should say themselves: what were they presuming to tell their colleagues? Why were they gathering them together to say it? Such a meeting was obviously not a "program," and in their vague imagining, neither Self nor Murphy had ever pictured very clearly how they might get from where they were—that is, in an institution with almost no cross-curricular work among faculty whatsoever—to the quasi-Writing Project program they hoped for. But the meeting was a start, and it felt to them like a good one, however it might develop. Then suddenly, after all their meeting and talking and thinking about writing across the curriculum, an entirely unexpected chance presented itself for doing something more elaborate at Radford.

In January of 1982, the faculty came back from Christmas vacation to a memorandum from President Dedmon announcing a special faculty convocation. Scheduled as usual for Porterfield theater, this meeting was unprecedented. Normally, Dedmon addresses the faculty only once a year, the weekend before fall semester classes begin. Rumors flew. The most confident prediction was that he was about to announce his resignation. But Dedmon laughed that off in an opening joke ("I might as well give you the bad news first: I have not the slightest intention of going anywhere."), and then got straight to business.

He wanted to propose two changes to improve both the academic character and reputation of Radford University. He wanted the faculty to consider them and, being diplomatically careful about jurisdiction, he wanted the appropriate faculty bodies to take what action they saw fit. But in characteristic fashion, he insisted that action was pressing, and by calling a special convocation, he gave his proposals dramatic force.

First, he argued that the entrance requirements to the teacher-training program at Radford should be raised. Radford University began, he reminded his audience, as a teacher-training institution, and it had assumed over the years a "historic and highly regarded role in training many teachers of the Commonwealth." Pointing to the decline in prestige of education programs and the recent calls for greater competence and professionalism among teachers, Dedmon proposed that Radford's teacher-training program institute a higher minimum grade point average for entering students. If such a policy were established, Radford would be "the first Virginia college or university—public or private—to implement demonstrably more rigorous requirements for entering the teaching field." It would be an important symbolic gesture, Dedmon asserted: "As quickly as this university makes it clear that it places the highest possible premium on excellence, even in its program admissions requirements, the popularity of teacher training will be significantly enhanced and increasing numbers of exceedingly able students will seek admission to the teacher-training program."

Dedmon's second proposal was more general. It did not call for a specific policy change, but it required, he said, "the dedicated attention of all of us in the faculty." It was to increase the quantity and quality of student writing throughout the undergraduate program at Radford University. Echoing the current public concern over poor writing by college graduates, Dedmon said, "I have grown increasingly worried about the quality of writing exhibited in the work of our students," and he went on to assert his belief that this trend could be reversed if all faculty at Radford assumed responsibility for student writing. He did not mean to call for greater penalties for poor writing, he insisted. Nor was he suggesting some sort of "minimal competency in writing" exam, a practice he would consider a "sad commentary on our instructional programs generally." Instead, he was calling for more attention to the teaching of writing. He cited the careful scrutiny his own teachers had given to his writing as a student, and the individual help they had offered him. He called on the Radford faculty to do the same: "In all courses possible, on all occasions possible, we must expand the opportunities for students to write and to be instructed in their writing efforts." He did not say how he thought such a goal could or should be accomplished, but he urged faculty to consider it their shared responsibility, and he asserted in closing that working toward it would demonstrate publicly Radford's commitment to academic excellence.

Neither Murphy nor Self had ever talked with the president about writing across the curriculum or their inchoate thinking about it. But the morning after the speech, Murphy walked over to his office to tell him how important a public statement he thought it was. The ideas Dedmon had articulated were those that Murphy had been introduced to in the Bay Area Writing Project and that he and Self had been exploring for nearly two years.

Dedmon listened. Then he made a suggestion. The University Foundation was just that spring instituting a series of small faculty-development grants. Perhaps some sort of program could be funded by one of these in-house grants.

When Murphy told Self of this suggestion, the two of them scheduled another meeting with the president and brought him a sketch of what a one-year introduction to writing across the curriculum at Radford might look like. Dedmon was supportive. Could money be gotten for printing, for refreshments, for consultant travel and honoraria? they asked. Tactfully—not being a member of the independent Foundation—Dedmon said that he could not be sure. But his tone seemed unmistakable, and he asked that the grant application be routed through his office, so he could add his endorsement to it.

The Writing Across the Curriculum program was granted $4000 for the academic year 1982–1983. This award amounted to two-thirds of all the money the Foundation had at that time to give. Even as they were writing the proposal, Murphy and Self thought it was ambitious. But they remembered the advice Dedmon had given them in his office—characteristic advice delivered with characteristic emphasis: "Don't think small."

Chapter Three

Writing Across the Curriculum at Radford

Radford's Writing Across the Curriculum program is presently being coordinated by eight faculty members from seven departments. Rosalyn Lester, the chair of the department of fashion design, is serving as head coordinator, overseeing its various activities and managing its budget. Bill Hrezo, chair of the political science department, and anthropologist Melinda Wagner have responsibility for organizing the two annual faculty weekend workshops. Charlene Lutes, a biologist and former Dean of the College of Arts and Sciences, and Pegeen Albig, a professor of dance, coordinate the writing-intensive courses. Recreation professor Lee Stewart plans and conducts the off-campus thesis workshop for graduate students and, with Sam Zeakes from the department of biology, schedules and arranges the on-campus faculty programs. English professor Susan Kirby coordinates program publications, the library, and faculty travel. The annual budget ($75,000 for the academic year 1991–92) provides stipends or reassigned time for these coordinators and funds off-campus faculty retreats, on-campus workshops, writing-intensive courses, faculty travel, teaching grants for faculty, and a writing workshop for graduate students.

One weekend each, during both the fall and spring semesters, a group of approximately twenty faculty attend an off-campus workshop on writing and learning. Each semester a dozen or so faculty offer writing-intensive courses. During the semester in which they teach these courses, faculty meet bi-weekly over lunch or dinner to discuss their goals and strategies, their students' writing, and their interim assessments of course progress. Early in the spring semester, an interdisciplinary group of graduate students are invited to an off-campus weekend writing workshop where, through tutorials, peer-group discussion, and extended periods of individual writing time, they are helped to work on their master's theses. Throughout the year, on campus, presentations by and for faculty are organized on a range of topics related to the uses of writing in teaching and learning. The program also earmarks a portion of its funds for faculty travel and in-house teaching grants. Outside the normal university travel budget, the Writing Across the Curriculum program makes expense money available to faculty who wish to travel to conferences, programs, or other universities to learn more about the relations between language and learning. And each year, some program money is made available to faculty to fund small, experimental teaching projects which link writing to their coursework in new ways.

In every way, this is a larger and more complex program than the one which began in 1982. Its leadership is greatly expanded. Its program offerings are much more varied. Its budget has grown to nearly twenty times that with which it began.

The initial $4000 that the university's foundation allocated for a one-year introduction to writing across the curriculum was enough to invite three well-known consultants to conduct workshops for Radford faculty—Lee Odell and Dixie Goswami in September of 1982, and Ann Berthoff in April of 1983. It also paid for the publication of a new faculty newsletter, *Writing & Learning,* and for the publication of a small booklet of faculty essays on writing for new students, called *Writing at Radford.* The bulk of that first year's activities, however—five panel discussions with Radford faculty—cost nothing. The panelists were asked to describe and discuss the ways they assigned and used student writing in their courses, and the whole faculty was invited (by photocopied fliers) to attend.

A second small faculty-development grant, this time for $3000, was received from the foundation to continue the program for the academic year 1983–84. This funding was sufficient to continue the newsletter and reissue *Writing at Radford* to all new students, as well as to invite Mary K. Healy to conduct a faculty workshop on campus. Five more panel discussions were held and reported in the program newsletter. The panelists from the first year were asked to expand their presentations into essays. These were collected into a photocopied book called *Working Papers on Writing and Learning* (1983) and distributed to all Radford faculty.

In the fall of 1984, a substantially expanded program was initiated, and the university began to fund it from its regular budget in the amount of $20,000 a year. This expanded program involved a

number of elements. In addition to continuing the regular activities of the first two years, Self and Murphy were granted reassigned time from teaching, one course each per term, to coordinate the program. Mary K. Healy was invited to conduct another campus workshop. Ken Macrorie and Nancy Martin also were brought to Radford to conduct faculty seminars. Videotapes of Healy's and Macrorie's workshops were subsequently edited, shown at conferences of the National Council of Teachers of English, and distributed through Boynton/Cook. Twenty faculty and administrators were invited to attend an off-campus weekend writing workshop at Pipestem State Park in West Virginia, and a collection of their writing—called *Writing from Pipestem* (1985)—was photocopied and distributed to the participants. Travel expenses were allotted for teams of faculty to visit other universities and attend writing-related conferences. And a special faculty library of books and monographs on writing and learning was instituted.

Regular university budget support for the program continued during the 1984–85 and 1985–86 academic years, but in early 1986 another expansion was proposed. The State Council of Higher Education announced that it would offer funding appropriations earmarked for special academic programs at public universities. Radford's Writing Across the Curriculum program requested additional funds for a series of twenty writing-intensive courses, released time for faculty teaching such courses, and stipends for those same faculty to attend week-long summer workshops for planning their courses and writing reflective essays about them once they had been taught. This—plus the regular, annual operating costs of the program—came to roughly $120,000 a year. The proposal was submitted to the state legislature in February of 1986 and approved that same spring for the two-year funding cycle that would begin July 1, 1986. In 1988, the program successfully renewed its application for special state funds, for a second two-year cycle, 1988–90. And in 1990, the state legislature again funded the program for the 1990–92 biennium.

While the name "Writing Across the Curriculum" has remained the same at Radford through these years of growth, the program itself has undergone substantial changes. Sometimes change has been driven by the amount and sources of funding. In 1983, for example, when the university administration agreed to take over (and increase) regular annual funding of the program, the coordinators had to imagine what such increased funding might be used for. The Commonwealth of Virginia provided a similar catalyst in 1986: what could the program do with four times the annual budget it had been using?

Sometimes change has been calculated. In order to make the program more truly cross-curricular, for example, the ideas and help of colleagues outside the English department were deliberately sought. Some of the most involved faculty were asked to assume central roles in the program's administration. When Toby Fulwiler visited Radford as a consultant in 1987, he argued that this was a tactical organizational mistake. But the program's coordinators were convinced that an across-the-curriculum program should be coordinated by an across-the-curriculum team, and continued to work toward radical collaboration in the program's leadership.

As calculated as such a development in program organization has been, it began by chance. In the middle of a faculty panel discussion, historian Richard Straw leaned over to Murphy and asked, "Why don't we have a panel discussion with students?" It was a good question, and since Straw agreed to coordinate such a panel, two changes began: (1) including students in faculty discussions of writing and learning and (2) involving other faculty in the coordination of program events.

The introduction of faculty weekend workshops began by a similar chance conversation. In the spring of 1984, driving Mary K. Healy to the airport for her flight back to Berkeley, Self and Murphy heard her extol the value of off-campus workshops. "Take faculty away," she said, "give them time to talk and write and think. That's what we've learned in the Writing Project. There's no substitute if you want people's minds to be changed." Because the coordinators were soon developing a proposal for expanded program activities, Healy's passing comment prompted them to include weekend workshops for faculty—a staple of the program ever since.

Faculty involvement in the program has itself been sometimes fortuitous. Bill Hrezo, for example, now the chairperson of the political science department, attended the first Writing Across the Curriculum workshop in September of 1982. He was not impressed. But he happened to be a friend of anthropologist Melinda Wagner. During a family dinner more than two years later, she encouraged him to reconsider the program. When Hrezo attended his next workshop, he found it very worthwhile, and he has been ever since one of the program's strongest faculty supporters. For two years, he served as editor of the newsletter, and for the past two years (with Wagner), he has coordinated the off-campus faculty workshops.

The Writing Across the Curriculum program at Radford has thus been characterized by change. It has also been characterized by informality in its structure. Its first organizers called themselves "coordinators," preferring that term to alternatives like "administrators" or "directors." It is housed in no office. After nearly ten years, it is still not possible to "find" the Writing Across the Curriculum program at Radford. The closest one can come is to find the person or persons who are currently serving as "head" coordinators. While Murphy and Self did most of the program administering, either one of them would do, but as more faculty have taken on coordinating roles, the need for someone to be named "head" has seemed more necessary. Yet the decentralized tradition of the program is so strongly established that even now the coordinators are reluctant to designate one of themselves as "head." And in any case, the title does not exist very far outside the circle of coordinators themselves; almost no one on the faculty knows who the "head" coordinator of the program is.

That is, the informality of the program runs deep in its character. It is felt to be ad hoc. Its participants have almost always sought to minimize its structure, even as it grew larger and more complicated. There are tasks to be performed. What are they? Who will do them? When? What help will they need? When the current coordinators gather during the early summer to plan for the next year, for example, they apportion the program's activities among themselves. They share their evaluations of past activities and rehearse their plans for the future. Everyone does what he or she wants to do and feels capable of doing well. Jobs rotate as individuals feel such a need. At the coordinators' meeting in the summer of 1991 for example, Susan Kirby, who had served as a "head" coordinator the previous year, chose to take over responsibility for program publications and budget. One of the two faculty who had been coordinating the writing-intensive course program, Rosalyn Lester, stepped in to assume the role of "head" coordinator.

During the early years of the program, Murphy and Self collaborated within just such a fluid structure. Several times a year, they would meet at a steak house away from campus for lunches that would last all afternoon. On napkins and placemats, they would sketch what needed doing and then sort out which of them would do which. Announcements needed to be prepared for the coming panel discussions. Videotapes of consultants' workshops needed to be edited. A site for the fall weekend workshop needed to be selected and reserved. Faculty to teach writing-intensive courses in the spring needed to be recruited. The budget needed balancing. The annual report needed to be drafted. These, and scores of incidental details, needed to be attended to, and responsibility for them all passed informally back and forth between the two coordinators. It would be an exaggeration to say that this was no structure at all, but it was as little as seemed possible. That little has always been regarded as provisional.

However informal its structure, since 1982, the Writing Across the Curriculum program at Radford has sponsored 95 faculty presentations in panel discussions. It has sent 90 faculty on program-sponsored travel to conferences and other universities. It has published 85 faculty articles in its newsletter. It has involved 250 faculty in off-campus workshops. It has engaged 80 faculty in teaching writing-intensive courses. In all, the program's activities have involved an estimated (most of these numbers are estimates; few exact counts have been kept) 300 teachers—nearly two-thirds of the full-time faculty.

These numbers suggest the considerable impact the program has had on the university faculty. But in its development, ironically, the program has been guided as much by the meeting of intuition and opportunity as by clear or settled purpose. Its growth has often been by chance, its evolution unexpected.

From their experiences in the National Writing Project and in the Virginia consortium, for example, Murphy and Self thought they knew what writing across the curriculum was and that they could deliver it to the faculty. But immediately they faced a dilemma: how could they offer their colleagues something they had not asked for and might not want, that is, more student writing? Murphy and Self knew that they did not want to presume to tell their colleagues what to do and how to do it. But then, how were they to proceed?

One solution was to hire outside consultants to come in and do the telling. That was only feasible on occasion. The program could afford only a limited number of consultants and for short visits. These consultants—Lee Odell and Dixie Goswami were first—turned out to be very helpful and their workshops valuable, but it was obvious that the program would need more than injections of outside ideas. So, from the start, as a matter of diplomacy, Self and Murphy asked their colleagues to say what *they* thought about writing in their courses, what *they* did with writing and why. Instead of being a transfer of information, then, the program took on unexpectedly the shape of a conversation.

In February of 1984, in preparing to ask the university for more regular funding than the foundation could provide, Murphy and Self told themselves that it should be brought into the mainstream of the academic program, that it should be "institutionalized," even though they had no clear idea what they meant by the term. They supposed that the university should support the program in its regular annual budget. With very little more than that to go on, however, they met at a local beer and sandwich shop and marathoned a brainstorming and planning session. Before they were done that night, they had sketched a "five-year plan." They collated their notes—placemats and napkins—talked over the general shape of their projections with a few colleagues, and then typed up a proposal which they sent to

Charles Wood, executive assistant to the president, and David Moore, then vice-president for Academic Affairs.

Self and Murphy asked for $20,000 a year. They urged the university to support the program even more emphatically than it had and for an extended period of time, not just year to year. They made far-reaching claims. What should Writing Across the Curriculum do? they asked. They invented an answer. As they described it in their proposal, the program should "contribute to long-term academic growth at Radford; provide opportunities for faculty growth and development; catalyze imaginative and intellectually rigorous innovations in teaching; [and] explore ways to embody such innovations permanently in the university curriculum." They felt brash; they considered their proposal daring. In it, they refused to promise quick or in any way quantifiable benefits. Rather, they insisted that the changes that should be expected at Radford because of this program would be slow, immeasurable, halting, and superficial. Then they added, with deliberate rhetorical spin, "radical": "The Writing Across the Curriculum program is essentially a teaching across the curriculum program: to consider deeply the problems of writing is to consider deeply the problems of knowing and learning, the most fundamental problems with which any teacher can be engaged."

Looking back on their proposal now, Murphy and Self think their approach was sensible and their claims sober. But at the time, they were made giddy with the thought that they had fabricated it all one long night in a restaurant, scribbling on whatever scraps of paper were at hand. In fact, they had been influenced by the ideas of many others and by the reports of program models at different institutions. But selecting from among those ideas and applying them to Radford required their own intuition and calculation—deciding to emphasize, for example, that the first objective of the program ought to be to encourage faculty writing, or asking the university administration to encourage and reward individual teachers for experimenting with ways to increase the quantity and use of writing in their courses. The light-headedness Murphy and Self felt was due to the light grasp they themselves had on what they were proposing. In retrospect, they now believe that they were patching together fragments of ideas without any explicit conception of the whole toward which they were working.

Another example—perhaps the most striking—of the fortuitous development of Radford's Writing Across the Curriculum program is the story of its writing-intensive courses. When such courses were first proposed in 1984, they were to be required in every undergraduate degree-granting program at Radford. The phrase "writing-intensive courses" was at the time becoming popular. Radford faculty had read about such courses at other colleges, among them U.C.L.A., the University of Michigan, and Yale. Such a university requirement, it was supposed, would help institutionalize Writing Across the Curriculum at Radford. It was not yet clear to anyone at Radford how such courses might be set up. It was not clear what they should look like when they were finally established. And neither Self nor Murphy had the doubts they would later develop about the wisdom of such a requirement. Still, they were proposed, and when, two years later, the Commonwealth of Virginia granted Radford's program a special budget appropriation, part of the money was designated for initiating writing-intensive courses.

When they received news of the state appropriation, Self and Murphy asked eight colleagues to meet with them off-campus for an extended and thorough examination of the Writing Across the Curriculum program, of the state grant, and of the writing-intensive course idea. It was an oddly timed meeting. The proposal had been submitted without these colleagues' consultation. The money was granted. Radford University was committed to writing-intensive courses. And *then* Murphy and Self asked for help. As it happened, however, the meeting was enormously fruitful. As a result of these colleagues' study and talk, the writing-intensive course "requirement" was scrapped in favor of the establishment of "pilot" writing-intensive courses. Provisional, like the program itself, all writing-intensive courses at Radford have since been "pilot" courses, experimental, exploratory. Faculty are invited to teach them for the opportunity they give to try out different uses of writing in their teaching.

But this meeting had a more important benefit as well. For the first time, the direction and purposes of the program as a whole were opened to the exacting scrutiny of a cross-disciplinary team of faculty. Before the four-day meeting was over, the program belonged to them all.

Not only have the structure and development of the program been fluid; its ideas themselves have undergone through the years a subtle transformation. Its purposes, the ideas it has publicized about writing and learning, even its focus on writing itself—all have evolved silently, but so importantly that the guiding ideas of the program in 1982 are radically different from the ideas of the program today.

The first program proposal submitted to the Radford University Foundation in 1982 emphasized the skills and processes students need to write successfully. The proposal echoed the university president's convocation call for more "acceptable" writing in every course at Radford. It also responded to strong media criticism at the time of the quality of student writing generally. Its objectives included a phrase about writing and learning—"to improve the quality of learning through writing for all Radford students"—but this phrase got little emphasis in practice. To teach students to write better and to teach them to use writing to help themselves learn better are two very different goals. It was years before either the coordinators or participants in Radford's program consciously registered the difference.

At Radford today, many observers still think the program is principally concerned with correcting student spelling and syntax and improving form. But for years, it has been concentrating much more strongly on the ways writing can be used to help learning. By the middle of the second year, for example, the program's five-year-plan proposal made no reference whatsoever to improving student writing. The president reflected this shifting emphasis in his own public notices of the program. In his 1984 convocation speech, he added a phrase he had not used before in discussing the importance of writing in the Radford curriculum. "Writing is," he said, "the tool of learning."

Correctness and writing well were not abandoned altogether. During the four-day advisory meeting at Pipestem in 1986, the participants vigorously debated whether writing-intensive courses ought to be designed to use informal writing to help students learn or whether they ought to be designed to teach students to write. The resolution of the debate was that the courses should do *both,* but four years earlier, when the program was just beginning, such a debate would have been impossible. The idea that writing might be useful for learning had not yet been clearly imagined.

The stated objectives of the program when it began in 1982 included one intended "to provide opportunities for faculty members to share with each other their approaches to teaching students how to write." Here again, the emphasis was on how to write. But this objective also mentions teaching, and in time *that* became a major preoccupation of the program, as well.

When Dixie Goswami conducted the first faculty workshop at Radford in September of 1982, she urged the participants to get together in small working groups to note and discuss the writing they thought their students actually did. As it turned out, no such working groups among faculty were formed. But in the panel discussions that were subsequently organized, a modified version of Goswami's idea was inadvertently implemented. As faculty shared their approaches to teaching writing, as they inquired into their own practices as teachers and examined stories of their own students' learning, they were undertaking (without knowing it) the sort of informal collaborative research Goswami had earlier recommended.

The subject of writing unfolded for them into questions about how to help students think and learn. Though such an expansion of emphasis had not been foreseen, it eventually appeared unavoidable. Talk about writing entailed talk about its purposes, about strategies for doing it, about criteria for responding to it—and all of these questions entailed larger questions of teaching: what are the course's purposes? what pedagogical methods can best serve those purposes? what can a teacher do to enhance students' learning?

This new attention to teaching and learning proved to be one of the strongest attractions of the program for many faculty. It is still one of the program's most important qualities. When Charles Wood was introducing it to the new vice president for Academic Affairs in 1989, this was the quality he pointed to. "It's been a very important program for a lot of faculty," Wood said. "It's been very helpful to them in their teaching." According to teachers like biologist Chuck Kugler, the benefit of the program for faculty interested in reflecting on and improving their teaching is incomparable. The Writing Across the Curriculum program, he says, is the only place on campus where faculty can come together to talk about education.

Kugler's own language, however, highlights a fundamental characteristic of Radford's program. It is actually no "place" at all. Its configuration is tentative, its ideas in flux. Because of the high visibility of its name and the generally favorable local impression of its success, it appears stable and tangible. But look more closely: it is a gossamer thing, a program of "opportunities," of dynamic moments of collaboration and insight.

Chapter Four

Moments of Collaboration and Insight

Since 1982, Writing Across the Curriculum has become one of the showcase features of Radford University. New faculty hear about it in orientation sessions and are urged to involve themselves in its work. At staff parties, social introductions often include the program affiliation of faculty who are serving as coordinators of Writing Across the Curriculum. After a year spent interviewing key members of different offices, departments, and colleges within the university, the new director of planning found it one program to which they all pointed as demonstrating the institution's academic accomplishment. When the university decided to develop a new emphasis on speech and oral communication in the whole undergraduate curriculum, it was to the Writing Across the Curriculum program that its first directors looked for a model and a precedent of success. Literature prepared for prospective freshmen by the Office of Admissions—for example, the 49-page glossy prospectus entitled "The Spirit of Change"—highlights the program as one of the distinctive signs of Radford University's character and aspiration. When the president was asked recently by the editors of the Alumni Giving Report to point to an academic program at Radford of which he is particularly proud, he immediately singled out the Writing Across the Curriculum program.

But as familiar as it is in name, what the Writing Across the Curriculum program actually is or does is less than clear, even to some faculty or administrators who have been at Radford during its entire life. Most assume that Writing Across the Curriculum is the same program it was when it began, just more firmly established and more visible. That is, the *name* of the program has assumed a character of its own in the university community, and the generally positive attitudes toward it persist almost independently of what it actually does.

Several reasons may help explain this apparently odd fact. First, the program has been in a nearly constant state of change, experimenting with different activities, reaching out to include different people, adapting to the shifting needs of the institution, and thus resisting permanence and fixed description. Second, the program's structure is largely informal. What is most visible of the program is the trace it leaves in personal anecdotes, newsletter reports, campus public relations information, and—at budget time—state funding decisions. Together with these is the growth of the program in fortuitous and unexpected ways.

But more important even than these reasons is the fact that Writing Across the Curriculum at Radford University is less a "program" than an "event." It fosters activities which are, by their very nature, ephemeral and whose operation in the minds of participating faculty and the culture of the institution is subtle and complicated.

In the spring of 1981, twenty-five faculty attended a meeting on the fourth floor of Young Hall to listen to Self, Murphy, and Kirby talk about writing. A follow-up meeting two weeks later attracted only five participants. The first faculty workshop—in September of 1982—billed with as much fanfare as the new program thought decent, featuring Dixie Goswami and Lee Odell, and very well-attended—so disappointed Bill Hrezo that he dismissed the program for three years. Peter Balsamo, the director of the university's continuing education program, attended a faculty weekend workshop in 1986 that he says now, five years later, was rich with teaching ideas for him and very valuable in providing him with personal contacts on the faculty. Melinda Wagner tells the story that in a chance conversation with Murphy in her office, her whole notion of what "term papers" in undergraduate anthropology courses might be was changed. Subsequently, Warren Self was so engaged by a presentation that Wagner and her students made to the faculty about a book of essays they had written for children that he enrolled in her ethnography course. It is almost an overstatement to call these "activities." They are bits of experience—permitted, arranged, triggered by the program—moments of collaboration and insight.

In its earliest years, the program was conducted personally and on foot. Its first coordinators met with individual faculty members, invited them to make presentations about the role of writing in their teaching and in their academic field, prepared photocopied fliers announcing panel discussions for faculty, and baked apple cakes and bought styrofoam cups for refreshment coffee.

When they heard in conversation that historian Harold Mann eschewed essay exams, they invited him to participate in a panel discussion to explain why. They heard by chance from students that Larry Terry, a management teacher, assigned lots of writing in his courses. They made an appointment with him, sat down in his small, neat office in Whitt Hall, asked what he was doing with writing, listened, and asked if he would be willing to describe one or two of his projects to a group of faculty from other departments. He said yes.

Nearly always, the faculty said yes. One reason for this, some have since noted, was the personalities of the coordinators themselves. "It's almost impossible to say no to Warren Self," comments Melinda Wagner. And this not because of any institutional authority or dogged persistence, but because Self's manner is so forthright. His requests, notes Lee Stewart, always seem personal, like a friend asking for a favor. He has a way of making a request that inspires confidence in your ability to contribute something of value. Mathematician J.D. Hansard describes Murphy's manner this way: "When Rich Murphy talks to you, he stands a little closer than is normal. He shakes your hand warmly and a little longer than is normal. He listens intently." With characteristic irony, Hansard says it was his colleague, not the ideas, that initially sold him on writing across the curriculum.

Whether because of ideas or persons, faculty said yes to the first invitations to participate in the program. Doug Brinckman from business law. Biologist Richard Hoffman on the "art" of writing science. Lin Young, Diane Birch, Maggie Bassett, and Susan Donckers—nursing professors explaining the essential importance of writing in nursing. Larry Hembroff on the disciplinary conventions of writing in the social sciences. Sometimes the presenters asked for help. They wanted to talk more about what to present and how. Either Self or Murphy met with them again, encouraged, helped them rehearse ideas to discuss. But once they had accepted the invitation, the faculty put upon themselves the obligation to do what many of them had never done before: to articulate to their colleagues (many of them outside their own fields) their ideas about writing and the principles and practice of their teaching.

The Writing Across the Curriculum program at Radford is, as much as anything else, a decade of such moments: individuals in conversation with one another, sometimes public, sometimes private, sharing their own ideas, challenging each other, learning, shaping the program themselves.

The day after each panel discussion, Murphy and Self always tried to remember to send a note of thanks for their colleagues' contribution to what they called the faculty "dialogue" about writing and learning. The word implied an ambitious claim, part desire, part description. In fact, the session may not have been well-attended. (An audience of twenty was a crowd; six or eight was a disappointment, but not uncommon.) The discussion may have been animated or not. But the coordinators were interested in more than the size of the audience or the vigor of the talk. They were working toward the development of a *sense* of ongoing conversation among faculty, even among those who did not participate directly. They were glad when someone—biologist Sam Zeakes or marketing professor Mac Banks—stopped in the hallway to say, "I enjoyed that session the other night; been thinking about it a lot." But they felt the program's purposes were being achieved even when they were waylaid by an apology: "I'm sorry I couldn't make it to your panel discussion last night; I meant to."

Another medium or catalyst for conversation was the program newsletter, *Writing & Learning.* Usually appearing six times a year, it was a labor-intensive project. When Warren Self first asked Susan Kirby to serve as editor of *Writing & Learning,* she didn't realize just how intensive the labor would be. A wife and mother raising two children, commuting an hour and a half daily, teaching a full load of classes, writing and publishing in professional journals, presenting papers at conferences—Kirby was already juggling an overfull schedule. Still, she agreed to take on the job. And for four years, she wrote, typed, and edited the newsletter. She laid it out, carried it over to the printing department, picked it up, stapled it by hand on the floor of her office, counted out piles for each department on campus, and delivered it to their mailboxes.

At the end of early issues, Kirby left space for faculty to write in suggestions or make contributions. Rarely did she receive any. Often she wrote most of the copy herself, announcing upcoming workshops, reporting on the presentations of faculty at the periodic panel discussions, quoting selected passages from reading she considered helpful:

Discourse does not just convey thought . . . it forges it.

James Moffett
(October 1982)

To understand is to invent.

Jean Piaget
(January 1983)

> One thing that is always with the writer—no matter how long he has written or how good he is—is the continuous process of learning how to write.
>
>   Flannery O'Connor
>   (October 1986)

Gradually, some faculty volunteered brief articles for the newsletter. Some were approached and asked to contribute their ideas about their own uses of writing in their classes. Some faculty who traveled to conferences or other campuses to learn about ways to incorporate writing in their teaching were asked to submit short essays to the newsletter reflecting on what they had seen and heard.

On one occasion, an actual exchange among writers occurred. Deborah Dew, an English professor, attended Georgetown's "Approaches to Teaching Writing" seminar in the summer of 1985. She came home critical of what she heard. She considered it passe, just a repackaging, she said, of the James McCrimmon "process" she had been using since she began teaching in 1963. She also considered it wrong, wasteful in its neglect of preliminary outlining:

> What . . . bother[s] me about the "new" approach to composition, as I hear people speak of it, is that students begin writing without knowing what they want to say and continue not knowing until the fourth or fifth draft, and they outline after they have written something to see whether it coheres. (*Writing & Learning* 4.4 [1986]:3)

Dew's complaint seemed directed at more than the Georgetown seminar. Implicitly she seemed to be criticizing the Writing Across the Curriculum program at Radford for its own apparent enchantment with the "new" approach of "process."

Warren Self wrote an extended reply for the same issue. Instead of addressing Dew's defense of outlining, he reframed her criticism as a complaint against putting a new label on old practices. Thus he was able to appear to agree with her, while at the same time claiming both that there were new ideas worth considering and that Radford's program was considering them:

> Debbie Dew is reminding us again that we must ever be careful to prevent phrases and superficiality from replacing substance and commitment. . . . In discussions at workshops and other meetings related to writing across the curriculum, Radford faculty have persistently asked tough questions about what effects on their teaching the adoption of the writing process approach would have. Those questions have stirred minds and resulted in extraordinary exchanges about what it means to teach, to learn, to compose, to think, to know. (*Writing & Learning* 4.4 [1986]: 6)

Such exchanges as this one between Dew and Self were rare. Only one other time did faculty use the newsletter for an exchange. Then, too, it implicated the program. After he had joined Kirby as co-editor, Kim Kipling introduced the March 1988 issue with a commentary on Allan Bloom's *Closing of the American Mind,* E.D. Hirsch's *Cultural Literacy,* and what Kipling called the "growing battle over educational reform." In itself, this would have been enough to elicit response, but Kipling credited writing across the curriculum (at Radford and elsewhere) with being on the progressive front lines against a reactionary movement to "return to a 'classical' curriculum and . . . to the 'great works and great minds' of the past" (*Writing & Learning* 6.5 [1988]: 1).

In response, political scientist Craig Waggaman wrote the only "Letter to the Editor" in the newsletter's many-year history. Not only did he criticize Kipling for apparently oversimplifying the debate over educational reform. He criticized Kipling's representation of the Writing Across the Curriculum program as well:

> WAC at Radford deserves to pat itself on the back occasionally— anything which brings teachers and students together in a dialectic about what teaching and learning is all about is OK with me. I am very leery, however, of any attempt by one program to appropriate for itself and its methodology the "right" definition of good teaching. There is an amazing variety of good ways to teach and to learn—and we should look for an approach towards good teaching which is positive and not exclusionary. (*Writing & Learning* 6.6 [1988]:5)

Kipling, a professor of philosophy, had agreed to become associate editor and to share with Kirby some of the duties of writing, soliciting, editing, and shepherding the newsletter into print. For two years, they worked together. Then Bill Hrezo took Kirby's place, and two years later, Kim Gainer, a new English professor, took over Kipling's job as associate editor.

The masthead, *Writing & Learning,* was chosen long before it was clear to anyone at Radford how emblematic it would be of the program's developing emphasis. The newsletter was comprised of two columns of compressed type, usually on both sides of two eight and a half by eleven sheets, stapled. It is likely that many faculty did not read it and that even among those who did, most did not read it all. Still, it served as a sign of the talk going on among faculty about writing across the curriculum; indeed the newsletter was itself one important vehicle of that "talk." J. D. Hansard never wrote back, but he says that the newsletter was one of the best features of the program. Kirby "never wrote a silly thing," he says. "She always made me think."

As vigorous and satisfying as the collaborative talk among faculty sometimes was, at other times it broke down. Sometimes, the only insight seemed to be of failure. Some faculty returned from presentations or workshops, for example, never to participate again. "A waste of my time," one said, having spent the weekend writing about topics he regarded as frivolous. Another reported that she found a workshop utterly commonplace. A prize-winning teacher and an accomplished writer, she reported that she learned nothing about writing or revising. The only new thing was the faculty she had the opportunity to meet; other than that, she said, "I was hearing things it seems like I knew—gosh—when I was born." One faculty member argued publicly that she couldn't, that she wouldn't, do the writing assigned in a workshop, that it was intellectually disreputable even to be so asked.

During one weekend meeting, a faculty member's personal writing triggered such an intense emotional crisis for him that he broke away from his colleagues to wander alone in grief and bitterness on the margin of the group. They tried to help him, to draw him back at meals or on walks, but with only slight success. In the final evaluation session of the workshop, however, he spoke out.

"I just want to caution you," he said, quietly, somberly. "What you are doing here is very dangerous."

For him, the experience of the weekend workshop was traumatic, but for many others the weekend workshops have been the most valuable part of the program. For seven years—at Mary K. Healy's suggestion—such workshops have been conducted for small groups of faculty at least once a year. To describe the way they actually work is to tell of more than the usual schedule of discussions about the writing process and assignment making and evaluation, interspersed with periods of individual writing and scheduled meetings of small writing groups. It too is a story of intense moments.

In the humid July of 1984, Murphy drove over into West Virginia with his seven-year-old son to look at Pipestem State Park, a possible site. They rode the gondola down the side of a gorge to Mountain Creek Lodge, and he tried to imagine what it would be like to bring a whole group of faculty into that seclusion. He could not picture to himself the scene that would play itself out four months later or anticipate the feeling that would prompt his newsletter account of the weekend:

> There was time . . . (if one rose early) for a walk along the Bluestone River or a run part way up the mountain. But mostly it was work— writing before breakfast, talking animatedly together through all the meals, refusing to take breaks even when there were breaks to be had (the discussions and arguments continuing on the balconies into the night and back in the rooms). It was an extraordinary

collegial experience—intensely personal, intellectually demanding, and professionally enriching.

    It rained a lot down in the Mountain Creek gorge. Then the sky cleared. The yellow of the tulip poplar leaves was brilliant against the blue. (*Writing & Learning* 3.3 [1984]: 1)

Weekend writing workshops have been held since at Pipestem, at Doe Run and the Peaks of Otter on the Blue Ridge Parkway, and at Mountain Lake in nearby Giles County. All expenses have been paid by the Writing Across the Curriculum program. Rooms have often been private, so participants can have a place to read and write alone. Participants are always incredulous. "You mean we can order anything on the menu?" Then, more often than not, they eat happily more than they should.

Full participation has almost always been required at Radford's weekend workshops. This has meant that no spouses or children can attend, and this in turn has meant accepting the fact that some faculty with dependents they can not leave will be unable to participate. In October of 1984, it meant telling Academic Vice-President David Moore in his office, with his wife Priscilla present, that, no, she could not come along.

At first, Murphy and Self were afraid that if they simply issued an open invitation to a workshop, no one would accept. So instead they created a list of faculty they thought might be interested, tried to make the list generally representative of the faculty as a whole (with participants from each of the five undergraduate colleges), and contacted each person individually, inviting him or her personally. They calculated that such direct contact would yield a higher acceptance rate. What they did not imagine was this: that many of the faculty who attended would feel privileged to be asked.

In journals they have written afterwards and exchanged among themselves, faculty have recorded their wonder at the workshops' spirit and value: "I have never had a more exciting or intense weekend of intellectual stimulation and exchange about teaching in my fifteen years in this business." "What I found most enjoyable at Pipestem was that everyone cared about teaching. No one was bored. (It was hard to be bored in such relaxing surroundings, with the beauty of the cabins, the creek, and the mountains; with the delicious meals; with the vibrant people)." "The memory that I have of the weekend that is most enjoyable is that everything I remember of it is positive. It was very gratifying to me to be in the midst of teachers who spoke enthusiastically and positively about their students and who were committed to learning new avenues of teaching them."

Before the final session of the 1984 workshop, a small group of faculty gathered at the edge of the Bluestone River for an impromptu rock-skipping contest. Among them was David Moore, the vice president for Academic Affairs. Warren Self had suggested that Moore be invited. Since he was the senior academic officer of the university, it would give the administration a first-hand view of what the program was up to. Still, including him as a participant in the workshop was risky. Murphy and Self feared that his presence might intimidate other faculty or dampen discussion, and if the weekend were a flop there would be no disguising the fact. As it turned out, Moore's acceptance of the invitation itself should have allayed their fears. He entered animatedly into the discussions, drafted an intimate essay about his boyhood relationship with his father, invited faculty to his room for late-night scotch.

An essential moment in the history of Radford's Writing Across the Curriculum program was the success of that weekend workshop for Moore. The next year, when an orientation reception was held for the faculty who would be attending the second weekend workshop, Moore was asked to speak to them, to briefly reflect on his experience. He left many things unsaid—the scotch, the rock-skipping, the essay about his father. What he did say was this:

"I'm not always going to be vice president for Academic Affairs, you know. One of these days, I'm going back to teach. And when I do . . . I'll tell you one thing: I'm going to be trying the things I have learned in this program."

Seven years later, he *is* back in the classroom, and when he thinks back over the program it is that weekend he remembers most distinctly:

> The thing I recall most vividly impacting on me was the result of that very first workshop at Pipestem. Really, for the first time in my life, I realized that writing was a way of learning. I had used writing in my own classes as a way to have students demonstrate to me what they had already learned. But I didn't use it as a way of teaching these students or having them learn something. I used it as a way for them to tell me what they had already learned. I realized at that very first Pipestem workshop back in the early '80s that you guys were trying to get a lot more than that done. That faculty really could use writing in their classes as a way to have students learn things.

The insight and intensity felt by many faculty who have attended weekend workshops are difficult to communicate. Sometimes, they come back to what they call the "real world" and cannot express their gladness or find it quickly dulled. Sometimes, their colleagues smile in disbelief at their enthusiasm. Certainly it is the case that many faculty at Radford still do not know about or understand or value what others of their colleagues regard as one of the transforming moments of their teaching careers. Some faculty scheduled to attend weekend workshops forget the dates, do not show up, call at the last minute to cancel (too late to replace them or to withdraw their room reservations). "Sorry," they say, "can't be helped. But if there's ever anything I can do for the program, be sure to let me know."

The benefits some faculty experience in a weekend workshop, others find concentrated in a writing group. Mike Dumin, for example, who teaches physical education, joined his first writing group in 1987. He had been supervising the fitness hour for faculty and staff at lunchtime in the Peters Hall swimming pool. He found himself telling someone that, though he had not actually done so, he had meant to participate in one or another of the Writing Across the Curriculum activities. Then he went back to his desk to find a call for proposals for writing-intensive courses. He applied, his application was accepted, and in due course he found himself both in a workshop for instructors of writing-intensive courses and in a writing group.

They met every other day for two weeks, reading drafts of their writing to one another and asking for help, feedback, suggestions, criticism. Mike Dumin was working on the proposal for a book he hoped to write on the experience of physical exercise. It was the first time he had ever participated in a writing group.

"I was LD in public school," he later explained. "Reading is still a struggle for me. I tend to look at the first letter of a word and guess. I guess that's one of the reasons I don't enjoy writing. In reading my own words, I know what I want to say and I see it, but it may not be there. I just fill in."

The group experience was surprisingly positive for Dumin. Instead of denigrating what he wrote, his colleagues looked at it, helped him see what he was saying, suggested ways to clarify and tighten. He had never encountered such help before. Usually, he admitted candidly, his colleagues have scorned his writing. Memos he has sent out have come back with errors circled and unfriendly notes. "Some people read for errors," he says sadly. More than that, their criticism has become personal, questioning his qualifications as a teacher. "Maybe you shouldn't be here," their replies to him have said. But in the writing group, Dumin encountered colleagues who would discuss his writing without personal animus: "You know they are talking about the writing but you know they are not evaluating you."

The effects on Dumin have been great. Because of his experience in writing groups, his motivation to write has for the first time in his life grown. What he learned in groups has also altered his teaching. An outdoorsman and an excellent coach, he had earlier focused his teaching primarily on class discussion of concepts derived from the reading and on skill development. He had rarely asked students to write at all. Now he structures more organized time in his courses for students so that their ideas and their writing can develop as his own has done. He also has learned—from observing the kind of feedback he has received from colleagues—to give students more helpful response to their writing, not just criticism but positive suggestions and a clarifying sense of purpose. Further, the collegial exchange he experienced in writing groups has inspired Dumin to spread it among his colleagues. When small in-house grants were offered for inter-disciplinary projects, Dumin applied for funds to bring faculty to-gether for a series of luncheon seminars on teaching and writing. He was trying to foster talk like the talk he had experienced in his writing group—attentive, thoughtful, positive. As a prompt for each lunch discussion, Dumin asked his colleagues to write.

Sometimes the moments of personal insight which have ani-mated Radford's Writing Across the Curriculum program have been, like Dumin's, concerned specifically with writing and teaching. Sometimes their scope has been broader. In May of 1987, for instance, a workshop was conducted on campus for faculty teaching writing-intensive courses. Thirty-eight faculty were participating. One morn-ing, in one corner of the room, an ad hoc group of six gathered to discuss James Britton's "Language and Learning" chapter from the Bullock Report.

The discussion exploded. Britton's conception of language, some said, undermined the political agenda of the Bullock report. In imply-ing a world which language merely reflected, they argued, Britton was adumbrating the positivist premises of education which his research group was trying to challenge. His own language itself was reactionary, one said, using words like "master" and "control" to describe a per-son's relation through language to the "world." What are we doing here in Writing Across the Curriculum, some asked, if it isn't to value the language of learners themselves in constructing the world?

It was an essential question—about the philosophy and poli-tics of the program itself, even about the felt experience of the persons in the group. If it was not finally answered, it left at least one trace in the journal of one of the participants, written later that afternoon:

> Got to write down my excitement—the thrill of our discussion this morning—analyzing/critiquing Britton's Bullock Report piece. I thought/said that one of the reasons I don't buy into the post-

modernist thing is that it seems to me to isolate us—saying that language does not contain referential meaning. But Glen said, no, just the opposite—and Marcella added: it's bringing us together. I was stopped and suddenly flashed on a feeling just a glimmer of union, a hint of communion among us that might be possible—Glen made me hope that there might be a world—if we could come to understand ourselves this way, if we could come to—what?—*use* language in this way?—

This journal entry ends in questions. The discussion that prompted it raised issues it could not resolve. The Writing Across the Curriculum program has provided the occasion for many such moments. Some say that one reason for the program's success is that it has not insisted on resolution. It has deliberately tried to avoid orthodoxy. Thus, at times, the faculty who have participated in it have found themselves in deep disagreement with one another. Sometimes these disagreements have been enough to drive faculty away from any further involvement in the program. At other times, disagreement has simply been accepted as the natural consequence of bringing together different minds. Sometimes difference has paradoxically intensified agreement and the sense of common purpose and community. Nowhere was this more evident than in the planning meeting conducted in May of 1986.

Ten faculty agreed to spend the week after graduation discussing the scope and direction of the program. In order to foster as open a discussion as possible, Murphy and Self tried several things they had not done before. In preparation for the meeting, they asked the participants to write about their own perceptions of the program's purposes and effects. They asked Richard Straw to chair the meeting. With him they drew up, from the writing of the participants, an agenda for the discussion.

They had already submitted a proposal to the Commonwealth of Virginia for the next two years and, in the form of a special appropriation from the state legislature, received a huge increase in funding. Suddenly, they felt that they should not be making all the program decisions alone. So they asked a small group of colleagues to help them think about where they were going.

When it was clear that the question was a genuine one, the disagreements flourished. One participant said the program ought to end, that it ought to be aiming to *make* itself obsolete. Another said that this was politically savvy since it certainly *would* end: the money would not last forever. Melinda Wagner spoke out passionately against letting the program dissolve. "We *need* it," she said, "to give ourselves permission to talk. . . . *I* need it." But when the discussion turned to administrative structures for ensuring the continued life of the program, one participant said, "I hate this." When the group tried to decide what they thought "writing-intensive" courses should be, the disagreement reached its sharpest pitch.

How much writing should they contain? What should the writing be for? How should such courses be advertised and scheduled? Among some of the participants, a consensus emerged that what they called "wic" courses should include both formal and informal writing and that they should *not* be specifically identified in the university catalogue or the schedule of classes. Two reasons seemed to lead to this last: (1) that the writing in these courses should be regarded as a means of instruction rather than as a part of the content and (2) that advertising courses as "writing-intensive" might drive students away from them and give faculty the impression that other courses did not need to include or use writing. This consensus prevailed, but not before it had convinced one participant—J. D. Hansard—that in fact he could not and would not teach such a course. And not before it had elicited from history professor Noel Eggleston the passionate ethical objection that students have a *right* to know what is being offered (and done) to them. For years Eggleston continued to maintain that position and, though he used an enormous amount of writing in his undergraduate history courses and helped to review proposed writing-intensive courses by other faculty, he never taught one himself.

As divided as the faculty at this planning meeting were over particular questions, their common interest in the program and the university gave them also a keen sense of collegiality. As soon as spring semester finals and graduation were over, they wrote and talked and argued with each other more intensively than any of them ever had before in their teaching careers. They ate and walked together. In the rain and mud of a May afternoon, they played volleyball and slipped and slid and laughed together. When the meeting's chairperson, Richard Straw, overslept the last morning and came late and groggy to the meeting room, they teased him unmercifully (and have not let him forget it since). And to that last meeting, one of the participants brought each of his colleagues a gift.

George Parish, professor of music, had argued throughout the meeting that for all their interest in writing, they could not disregard their obligation to what he called "content." Every second-year theory student in his course, he would repeat, *must* learn what an augmented sixth is. Period. His was not the prevailing view of the group. But his idea was heard, more than that, welcomed as part of the unfinished discussion of what teaching and learning at Radford should and might be. And the respect with which these faculty regarded one another was epitomized in Parish's culminating gesture.

On nine pieces of staff paper—*his* writing paper, Parish said; he never goes anywhere without it—he sketched for each of his colleagues a different augmented sixth. One from the last movement of Mozart's 41st Symphony. One from Brahms, another from Aaron Copland. Each of them was chosen because the composition from which it came reminded him in some way of the person to whom he was giving it. In that surprising and elegant gesture he personalized a public theme. And in those gifts to his colleagues he provided a token of the complex ways Writing Across the Curriculum at Radford has challenged and rewarded the teachers who participate in it.

Chapter Five

Faculty Writing and Learning

George Parish was among the twenty participants at the first weekend workshop sponsored by the Writing Across the Curriculum program. It was October of 1984. At three o'clock on a Friday afternoon, seventeen faculty and three administrators gathered in the parking lot at the main campus entrance where two state vans and a station wagon waited. The vice president for Academic Affairs was there and the dean of the College of Business and Economics. There were teachers of mathematics and biology, English and history, sociology and business, education and nursing. Many of the participants had never met one another before. Even George Parish, who had been at Radford for fourteen years, was acquainted with only half of the colleagues with whom he would be spending the weekend talking, writing, and thinking about the uses of writing in learning.

Parish, the sole representative of the College of Visual and Performing Arts, was skeptical about the value of this undertaking, particularly for a discipline like his. Loading his suitcase into the back of the van for the two-hour journey to Pipestem, he was entertaining second thoughts about this venture, thoughts that only later would be publicly voiced: "Why write about music at all? . . . Music is a language system of its own. . . . We learn music by listening, performing, composing . . . writing music, not *words* about music."

It was as a skeptic that George Parish entered the conference room that Friday evening for the opening session of the workshop. Reflecting on the weekend experience several years later, Parish wrote, "I suspect that among the people there I expressed reservations more consistently than anyone about the nature of the program as I understood it then." Even this was an understatement.

Not a man known for his reticence, Parish volunteered at several points during the weekend discussions that when he was a student, his professors had no mercy. All they were concerned with, he said again and again in different ways, was the finished essay. And all they wanted was that it be good, capital "G," underlined, *Good*. If it weren't, he said, they would throw it back at you, along with a few insults for good measure. "You're wasting my time with this," they would say. "Get out, get out," they would shout at their trembling students, "out of my office with that tripe. And don't come back until you've written something respectable."

These were George Parish's teachers at the University of Michigan in the early 1960s. One of them, the most fierce, was the director of his research and dissertation. The anecdotes Parish was telling his faculty colleagues that weekend were his own stories. He would bring his writing to his teacher and try to brace himself for the thundering reaction—and when he told the story, he made his own voice imitate that remembered thunder—"C-R-A-P!"

The workshop leader, Mary K. Healy, was introducing ungraded, informal writing to these twenty Radford teachers. It was a new and alien planet in George Parish's heavens. To consider using writing to think or explore or wonder about a phase in the history of opera seemed to challenge Parish's whole experience of what writing in school could be and could be used for. And as painful as his own experience of writing in school had apparently been, the new approaches to writing that he was introduced to that weekend were equally disturbing.

Just how disturbing became clearer on the following Monday morning. One of the Writing Across the Curriculum program coordinators had stopped by his office to visit. Parish began to rehearse again, and more vehemently than he had ever voiced them in the workshop, his grave reservations about the implications of what he had heard. The emphasis given to "first-draft" writing implied in his mind a denigration of final-draft writing. The invitation to students to speculate about Monteverdi seemed very near to abdicating one's responsibility to teach the facts of music history such as that the first modern opera, *Orfeo*, was composed in 1607.

Denigration. Irresponsibility. Parish paced back and forth in his office, animated, re-invoking the images of his mentors, of the teachers who had not only terrified him with their standards but taught him thereby how to teach.

When he wrote later—he often wrote to the program coordinators after one or another Writing Across the Curriculum function he had participated in—to thank them for inviting him to participate, he called what he had heard a "revolution." That's what it actually boils down to, he said, a revolution in teaching. In a later note he expanded on this early insight: If I take what I'm hearing in Writing Across the Curriculum and try to apply it in my own classroom, I'll have to change completely the way I teach. And (he added parenthetically) I don't know if I ought to do that.

Historian Richard Straw was beginning his fourth year at Radford when he was invited to the same weekend workshop in 1984. Describing himself as one "predisposed to innovation and change," Straw says he was an eager participant in what he then saw as an experimental program.

Like Parish, Straw heard Mary K. Healy talk about the uses of writing as a mode of learning. "I heard," says Straw, "about a way to teach through writing that I had never encountered. Of course, historians write and I had up till then used essay exams exclusively, assigned term papers, book reviews, and other types of formal writing. But at Pipestem I heard something new, call it writing-to-learn, informal writing, free writing, expressive writing; it was different."

While Parish described what he had heard as troublesome, disturbing, even dangerous, Straw describes it very differently: "At that weekend workshop I was introduced to a philosophy and an approach to teaching that I found challenging, fascinating, and exciting. I knew I had lucked into something that would change my fundamental beliefs about teaching, learning, and students."

As Richard Straw tells it, that change in beliefs began immediately: "I learned that I could use writing in my classes to do much more than simply evaluate students' understanding of course content. Writing, I discovered, could be used to introduce new information to the class, to stimulate creativity in classroom discussions, and to give students an outlet to express their feelings, frustrations, and concerns with me, the class, or the readings. Writing could also be an effective way to stimulate questions from the students and it could be used introspectively by them to assess the process of learning itself."

On the Monday morning following the workshop, Richard Straw walked into his American history class and spent the first half-hour telling his students what he had done over the weekend. Then he began to put these new ideas into practice. His students spent the next ten minutes writing a response to the day's reading assignment—the *Autobiography of Benjamin Franklin*—and the remainder of the period discussing issues that their writing had uncovered.

On the other side of campus George Parish was pacing back and forth in his office reflecting on the implications of this writing-across-the-curriculum business. The questions Parish raised at the workshop, and raised again that Monday morning, were matters of deep personal concern to a man who had practiced his profession for well over a decade and had established himself as an effective and respected teacher.

Parish's conception of himself as a teacher was not atypical, nor was his way of teaching. "I saw my main role," said Parish, "as lecturer and authority of last resort on any question relating to the class." He taught his students as he had been taught—by giving lectures, demonstrating principles, disseminating information. Describing his standard procedure in a music theory class, Parish stressed again his conviction that one learns music by writing music, not words about music, by studying music itself, not words written about music. "If I want students to understand the resolution of the secondary dominant seventh chord," explained Parish, "[I] show them how Mozart or Bach or Beethoven resolved those chords . . . . Similarly, if I want them to understand the multi-leveled nature of a tonal composition I show them a three-layered reductive chart, play each layer to confirm its relationship to the piece, and then—using my chart as a model as well as some basic concepts presented in the lectures—have them construct similar graphic analyses." Given such complex material and so much to cover in a semester, Parish had serious doubts about the practicality and legitimacy of introducing writing activities into his classroom.

He was not alone. Julein Axelson, a professor of foodservice management with teaching experience at three universities and many years of professional experience as a dietician and hospital foodservice manager, echoed many of Parish's concerns. "When I began hearing about Writing Across the Curriculum at Radford University," she said, "nothing about the program seemed to apply to me or my teaching: in fact, I resisted any personal involvement. I was interested in this movement, but only from a distance. I thought, 'Finally the university is doing something to improve students' writing' . . . but I didn't know how to teach writing, so this program had nothing to do with me. After all, my students had to 'learn the facts' in foods and nutrition and 'learn how to manage' in foodservice management. I didn't have time to spend on writing in my classes."

Like George Parish, Julein Axelson saw her role in the classroom as a dispenser of information, a presenter of facts. To accomplish this, she said, "There was only one way—lecture, interspersed with my spoken questions in an attempt to stimulate discussion or at least keep the students alert."

Axelson sensed that the principles and practices of writing across the curriculum, as it was evolving at Radford, posed a challenge to traditional pedagogy. Like Parish, she felt that writing across the curriculum implied an abdication of one's responsibility to teach the facts, to "cover" material.

This concern was shared by many. In fact, at that first weekend workshop, such reservations about what George Parish had called a "revolution in teaching" became public themes. Assuming the role of friendly curmudgeon, Parish deliberately impersonated his own teacher—"C-R-A-P"—in order to make the rhetorical point that there were powerful alternative views to consider. He made his natty clothes—starched shirts, polished penny-loafers—a public statement about teaching with discipline and with respect for finished performance. He chose a phrase or a fact—for example, that every second-year theory student in his course must learn what an augmented sixth is—and made it so resonant that it took its place as one of the idioms of faculty group conversation. Like "crap," his colleagues began to take up the phrase "augmented sixth" as embodying the irreducible content of the curriculum which teaching should not be allowed to neglect.

The fear of sacrificing content to a dubious experimentation with process was not what kept Karma Castleberry from participating in the Writing Across the Curriculum program in its early years. Of course, Castleberry, a professor of nursing, knew that she had to cover a great deal of material in her classes, that she had to prepare her students for the state administered examinations. But she, like Richard Straw, was prone to experimentation and innovation. In fact, it was her openness, her experimental bent, among other things, that made her such a popular teacher. Repeatedly, Castleberry had been nominated by her students for Radford's annual teaching award and, in 1981, the year before the Writing Across the Curriculum program officially began at Radford, she won the award for excellence in teaching.

Castleberry's reluctance to get involved in the Writing Across the Curriculum program was based on an assumption widely shared by faculty at Radford. As Castleberry tells it, "The WAC program had been around and I was always getting announcements of their activities in my mailbox along with the student foodservice menu. Both seemed to arrive around the same time and were printed on colored paper. I avoided looking at either menu; I figured WAC would be a diet of comma splices, split infinitives, and words like 'genre.' " Castleberry assumed that Writing Across the Curriculum was a program devoted to teaching grammar skills, a sort of composition-across-the-curriculum program intended to promote more elegant student prose and relieve the English department of the sole responsibility for teaching writing.

Despite this assumption, Castleberry's concern with her teaching and with her students' learning led her to accept an invitation to attend a weekend workshop in 1985. In an essay written two years later, she looks back on her concerns as a teacher and reflects on the motives that led to her involvement in the program:

> I was having trouble in my teaching again and no one took it seriously but me. I'm generally thought of as a pretty good teacher. When I complain about being bored and how the electricity in teaching is near a power outage, I get the usual etiological comments: you're just tired because it's the _____ of the semester (insert 'beginning,' 'middle,' 'end,' or designate the week, such as 'the fourth week').
>
> And then I got other advice about my teaching. Rather than dealing with etiologies, this advice was prescriptive: teach a graduate level course, do some research, or get involved in consultation. (These will revitalize an ailing academician.) So I did all of those things with relative success. There was a persistent gnaw of infidelity; I was hired to teach undergraduates. The other roles that I assumed treated symptoms, not the cause. I was still left with concerns about teaching . . . how to get students to tune in . . . how to foster their creativity . . . how to help them see things differently . . . how learning comes about.
>
> I wanted to talk about teaching with my colleagues without getting formula for writing behavioral objectives or hung up on how to number the parts of the official course syllabus. I didn't want to hear about how students aren't as bright as they used to be. . . . In the middle of one of those 'what am I doing teaching?' moments, I got an invitation to spend a weekend in a Writing Across the Curriculum workshop. I probably said 'yes' to the workshop because I was bored in the spring and the workshop wasn't until fall. ("Teaching-Writing-Thinking-Learning," 1987)

It was not boredom or low energy or self-doubt that led many of Radford's new faculty to the Writing Across the Curriculum program. More often than not, it was just the opposite.

Radford University was growing rapidly in the early 1980s. In a period of five years, enrollments jumped from 5,700 to 7,000. And in a single year thirty-eight new faculty were hired. They came from schools with reputations for academic excellence—Berkeley and Stanford, Chicago and Notre Dame, Duke and Penn State. These new faculty members were young and eager, ready to share their knowledge and advance their careers. One of the new recruits in 1984 was Kim Kipling, hired as an assistant professor of philosophy. Kipling came to Radford from Penn State where he had recently received his degree in philosophy and had taught courses in composition as an instructor in the English department.

Kipling began his career at Radford, he now says, with the exaggerated confidence of a new graduate: "With a doctorate in hand, some years' experience as a graduate student teaching critical thinking skills to rooms full of students in introductory logic classes, and two years' experience as an instructor of freshman composition, I felt quite confident in my own learning and in my ability to teach others something of importance."

Like most college faculty, Kipling had never been trained as a teacher; he had never taken a course in educational methods. He learned to teach, he says, by "becoming a voyeur, watching the masters at work."

"My professors," says Kipling, "were renowned scholars with vitae weighty enough to require extra postage—page after page of articles, books, and presentations to their credit. In the classroom they were impressive, lecturing with an air of authority and, on occasion, accepting a question from a courageous student. We listened. We took notes. And we wrote papers demonstrating our mastery of the material. Eventually the papers would be returned with a grade scribbled on the back, and sometimes a word or two—'Good,' or 'You should read Klossoski's latest article on this.' "

As a graduate student Kipling had taught several sections of a logic class. "I imitated my mentors," he says. "With all the confidence I could muster, I lectured to my students. I administered exams; I gave these exams to my assistant to grade." Later, as a teacher of English, Kipling instructed his students in the principles of rhetoric, the rules of grammar, the elements of style. "My students performed well," he says, "and I felt successful as a teacher."

For Kipling, the implicit assumption that Writing Across the Curriculum was a sort of expanded composition program served not as a deterrent but as an attraction. "In October of my first semester," he says, "I received a notice in the campus mail about an upcoming workshop sponsored by a program called Writing Across the Curriculum. I figured that this was something I might find interesting as a way of continuing my involvement in composition theory while also meeting some of the faculty from the English department. I asked my department colleagues about this program and discovered that they had heard of it but did not know what it was about. I thought I knew what it was about; I thought that there would be a discussion about developing a program like the one I had been a part of at Penn State, adding more writing courses and gearing them toward the kinds of writing characteristic of the various disciplines—Writing in the Humanities, Writing in the Sciences, Business Writing. I thought that my experience would enable me to make a contribution to such a discussion."

The workshop was conducted by Ken Macrorie and was titled "I-Search: Writing to Learn." Attending the workshop were faculty from a wide range of disciplines, as well as secondary school teachers and administrators. "Despite the peculiar make-up of the group," says Kipling, "I assumed that we were there to talk about composition, and I was prepared to do that. I was surprised to discover we were asked to write, to write and to read our writing to others. We wrote about our own learning experiences and about the kinds of things we, personally, would be interested in learning and how we would go about acquiring this knowledge."

Macrorie encouraged the participants to drop their masks as experts and professionals and assume the role of learners. He spoke about a revolution going on in some classrooms where teachers worked alongside their students on assignments, doing the writing themselves that they asked their students to do. "That suggestion," says Kipling, "struck me as astonishing—it challenged my notion that the classroom was a place where professors present information and students listen, record, and take exams on that information. Macrorie asked us to think of the classroom, the lecture hall, in terms of a learning environment, to think about the kind of climate we create. He asked us to think about learning."

Kipling left that afternoon workshop intrigued and troubled: "I wandered back to my office thinking about what I had heard—collaboration, climate, learning—about how little I knew about my business, how little thought I had actually given to the nature and process of learning." In an effort to clear up the confusion, he began to attend, more and more frequently, the functions sponsored by the Writing Across the Curriculum program—panel discussions, presentations, workshops.

Shortly after Macrorie's visit, campus workshops were conducted by Nancy Martin and Mary K. Healy. Kipling attended them all. In Healy's workshop, entitled "Creating Autonomous Learners," Kipling heard what sounded like a description of his own teaching practice. For the most part, said Healy, classroom writing has been considered important only as a way for students to show they *have* learned something. "The traditional strategies of class notes and essay tests," said Healy, "are largely dependent upon and directed toward the teacher rather than the student as an individual and autonomous learner." What she advocated instead was using writing as a *means* of learning. Healy described a number of strategies for using first-draft writing to engage students actively in the formulation and reformulation of knowledge.

Kipling began to reflect seriously on his own practice. He began, too, to experiment, transforming his own classroom into an arena where writing, discussion, and collaborative projects replaced lectures and note-taking. Looking back on his own development and the development of the program that year, Kipling says, "We began by discussing the kinds of writing students were doing in our classes, the kinds of assignments we were giving, the kinds of feedback we were providing our students. It soon became clear what Nancy Martin had meant when she spoke to us in November about the enormous potential for change that writing across the curriculum represents. She had warned that talk about writing was really talk about teaching, and talk about teaching was talk about learning. I saw that what was going on here was a collective effort to think about what it is that we—teachers and learners—are about."

Kipling was anxious to join his colleagues for the 1985 weekend workshop at Pipestem. Karma Castleberry was not. Her heart was still disengaged from teaching, she says; "hardly a flicker of passion remained." She was late for the pre-weekend faculty gathering to discuss the agenda, but when she arrived, she was surprised at what was taking place. "It didn't take long," she says, "to figure out that this wasn't a writing workshop about semicolons, but a workshop about teaching and learning. And I was smitten."

During the weekend, she discussed issues of teaching and learning with faculty from fifteen different disciplines. She read and commented on student essays. She talked about her own classroom practices. She drafted, revised, and read to the group a reflective essay about lingering memories of her first-grade teacher.

Castleberry describes the attitude she brought back this way:

> I wondered why no one had said that writing was about learning? Or, maybe they did and I never heard. I talked to a friend that night with the frenzy of a new convert. I talked about the writing-thinking-learning connection . . . how writing requires choosing forms and meanings . . . how writing is an act of commitment . . . a presentation of the self and one's thought . . . promoting reflection and scrutiny. I kept talking about the powerful effect writing and sharing were having on me. I fantasized what I'd do in my next classes . . . on Monday. I realized it had been some time since I'd felt that surge of excitement about teaching. I went to sleep wondering if it could last.

Since 1985, Castleberry has been an enthusiastic participant in Writing Across the Curriculum activities and a strong advocate among her colleagues at Radford and elsewhere. Despite the fact that it is school policy not to confer the teaching award on a previous recipient, Castleberry's students regularly recommend her for the prize. The reason may be gleaned from her own account of one of her recent classes:

> Here it is, full circle: I write to my students; they write to me and to each other. We share experiences and meanings through the

medium of language and somehow in that interactive process, everything gets transformed and changed. Which means we learn. Me, included. Everyone writes in this class; everyone is heard. Everyone discusses in this class; everyone counts. I grin to myself and remember what it was like to go through the moves in teaching, to have classrooms where only the most assertive students' voices were heard. I used to wonder if the silent majority thought at all. Now I hear every voice and read every voice. I know more about their thinking. I know more about my teaching. And we're both learning more about our individual and collective learning.

It was just two years before her retirement that Julein Axelson's interest "from a distance" in the Writing Across the Curriculum program was translated into personal involvement. Encouraged by her colleagues, Axelson volunteered to teach her Introduction to Foodservice course in the spring of 1987 as a writing-intensive course. As part of the agreement, Axelson met regularly to discuss problems, concerns, and successes with a group of faculty from various disciplines who were also teaching such courses. The weekly meeting, says Axelson, "was a seminar in the true sense of the word. The topics we discussed originated with all of us, sometimes announced beforehand, but often introduced at the meeting. We all contributed to the discussions. Sometimes the subjects for discussion were entirely new to me. I had never thought of them before. But they always stimulated me to examine my teaching. I found myself thinking more and more in terms of how students learn instead of in terms of how to teach."

Teachers of writing-intensive courses were asked to keep a log in which they recorded observations and speculations about the courses they were teaching. "My early entries," notes Axelson, "were filled with comments about the writing experiences in the class. Before long I was writing about the entire classroom experience. This approach, sitting down after class to write, was entirely new to me. It forced me to analyze each class, not just mope or gloat and hope the next class period would be more productive. As I prepared for the upcoming class, I found myself trying to figure out how to improve the learning situation or to incorporate what had worked well—a real change from my old style."

Julein Axelson, a college professor for 20 years, found that her classroom practice and her conception of her role as a teacher were transformed through participation in the Writing Across the Curriculum program. So did Moira Baker, a specialist in Renaissance literature, who joined the Radford faculty in the fall of 1986. Baker had just received a doctorate from the University of Notre Dame; she had come to Radford for her first full-time teaching position.

In the middle of her first semester, Baker, like all Radford faculty that year, received an invitation to submit a proposal for developing one of her upcoming classes as a writing-intensive course. She responded. Before the new semester began she met with a group of her colleagues, including Julein Axelson, to discuss and to plan the courses they would be teaching in the spring.

As she began to talk with her colleagues and to plan her course in Seventeenth-Century literature, Baker found herself exploring fundamental questions, questions she thought she had previously answered but which were now, in this dialogue with her peers, engaging her again. "What does it mean to 'know' the Renaissance? What does it mean to 'teach' the Renaissance? What do I mean when I ask students to 'learn' the Renaissance, when I say my hope for them is that they 'master' the Renaissance? For that matter, what does it mean to 'know' and to 'teach,' to 'learn' and to 'master' anything?"

Throughout the semester Baker kept a teaching log to record her responses to the class, and she met regularly with the faculty group to continue the dialogue about writing and the meaning of teaching and learning. At the end of the semester, during a week-long workshop, she wrote an essay reflecting on her experience and the experience of her students, for "their story," she says, "is my story."

As this was to be a writing-intensive course, Baker included a wide variety of writing activities in the course description she passed out to her students: a reader's log in which to annotate and respond to the texts, impromptu in-class writing exercises, an extended research project, and essay mid-term and final exams. "I hadn't anticipated," she says, "the impact writing would have on my relationship with students as they grappled with their own thinking. A lively dialogue sustained by their writing and my responses to them drew me more intimately into their learning process."

Baker's students used their daily logs to think their way through questions, to unpack dense metaphorical language, to explore ambiguities and paradoxes in the texts being studied. In reading these logs, Baker says, "I would sometimes see a desperate 'Help!' with a scowling 'happy face' sketched beside it. Sometimes a student would note a passage that was unclear to him or her, try to untangle it, and then give up. There was no way that I could *not* know how students were comprehending the material they were reading."

But if students' log entries sometimes ended with a plea for help, they also sometimes ended on a different note. Following an annotation on Ben Jonson's "Epigram 11," one student wrote: "Too often language that I don't understand frightens me—it has scared me away from plenty of poetry. Ben Jonson's language seemed unfamiliar at first; but, as I annotated the poetry it became under-standable, even enjoyable."

As the semester progressed, Baker found that more and more frequently her students were able to reach answers to their own questions in the process of writing responses to the texts. And often, too, the students' journal reflections, read to the class, took the place of the "teacher's" formal lecture. "By sharing the responsibility for class in this way," says Baker, "I hoped that I could convey to my students that we all have much to learn from one another."

Certainly Baker learned much from her students. She learned that her initial concern with "coverage" of material was misplaced, that she needed to pare back her syllabus to allow students more time to talk with one another, to work together on the material. A note from one student triggered a reexamination of the course plans:

> I'm getting a little confused. We do these poets so fast. I think it's great all the work we do and the intense focus we have, but some-times I'm just so overwhelmed that I can't keep Greville straight from Herbert straight from Herrick (I'm exaggerating of course, but . . .). I really enjoyed Donne—we spent plenty of time with him and he's my favorite. Others, however, aren't really as clear and I think it's because we didn't spend as much time with them. I *know* we have many, many major people to cover and I'm excited about them, but I still get bogged down and a little confused about who's who and who did what . . . .
>
> I hope this doesn't seem too complaining. I really just wanted to express a concern I was feeling with the class work and objectives.

Baker asked this student to share his concerns with the class, and in the ensuing discussion a number of other students expressed the same anxiety. "It was clear," says Baker, "that we had to do some-thing." And they did. Out of the syllabus went Thomas Adams. Out went Jeremy Taylor. Out went *'Tis Pity She's a Whore.* "I was learning from my students what it was I ought to be teaching," Baker says. "They, indeed, wanted to learn about seventeenth-century literature: they wanted to think about it more, to take it more fully into them-selves and have a coherent sense of what it is all about. It seemed to me that students needed the opportunity to talk more about the literature and to hear more of it. . . . Fuller class discussions took over the time relinquished by Thomas Adams and Jeremy Taylor."

Heartened by the quality of her students' work in their logs and in their class discussions, Baker prepared what she considered to be a challenging mid-term exam that would afford students the oppor-tunity to use their critical thinking to analyze individual texts and synthesize their insights about several texts.

The results were discouraging. An entry from her teaching log reveals her disappointment:

> Some students answered the questions only partially; some gave what appears to be half-hearted efforts. . . . I'm not certain what happened, but something is wrong here. I thought the exam was challenging, but certainly within the students' reach. Maybe I was wrong. Students were expected to explore the texts independently and to synthesize their thinking in original ways. I'd say over half the class could not do so with any degree of success.

Baker devoted the following class period to a discussion of the exam. She listened to what her students had to say and began to understand more fully what the problem had been: "I had assumed that they could take the step to synthesis on their own. And I had assumed that this kind of thinking would be familiar to them since most were juniors and seniors. The problem seemed so simple and self-evident now, that I don't know how I ever could have made the mistake in the first place: I had held students accountable on the exam for thinking skills which they had had neither adequate guidance in cultivating nor sufficient opportunity to practice. They had had to pay for my mistake, and I felt terrible about it. I felt as though I had pushed a non-swimmer into frigid water and yelled: 'Go on, swim! All you have to do is move your arms, and legs, and head like this!' "

Baker decided to share her analysis of the problem with her students: "Truthfully, I had never felt so vulnerable in front of a class as I did when I admitted that I had made an error in such a fundamental matter." Baker says the discussion had positive results: "The whole experience brought us closer together as we shared the difficulties of both learning and teaching."

Out came the scissors again. Out went more texts from the syllabus. In her lecturing and facilitating of class discussion, Baker began much more consciously to call attention to the kinds of thinking they were doing. She designed several in-class exercises that would involve her students in small group discussions followed by writing to engage them in the kind of thinking she wanted to help them learn how to do.

This focus on thinking skills paid off. Her students' performance on the final exam, reports Baker, revealed a new habit of mind that strained toward complex analysis and synthesis. And their term papers displayed an impressive comprehension of seventeenth-century literature. In fact, two of the students in the class had their term papers accepted for presentation at the Conference on Undergraduate Research at the University of North Carolina.

Baker drove them to the conference, and she remembers what it meant to them—"how proud they were of their own accomplishment, how confidently they shared their ideas and words with students from across the country." It was a moving experience, says Baker, "to watch these students step to the podium in full command of the situation, their thoughts and their words and their persons reflecting a joyful mastery of it all."

Moira Baker, and the colleagues with whom she shared her questions and discoveries, learned much from these students about the meaning of teaching and learning—and community. In the final lines of the essay she wrote for Radford faculty about this experience, she captures something of the essence of these meanings:

> I am asking my students not simply to 'gather and consume' course material, though gather it they must. I am asking them not simply to spin abstract theoretical webs, though theorize they must. It strikes me that I am asking my students to make their learning a part of their lives, to confront a bewildering array of information and theory, to take it into their minds, and to transform it into something entirely their own, something they have discovered and care about, something in which they invest themselves. . . . It is my hope that both my students and I may become this kind of learner. (" 'This Gift of Celestial Honey,' " 1987)

While Moira Baker sat at her computer recording these reflections on her experience and the experience of her students in the spring of 1987, Julein Axelson was in her office reminiscing about her teaching career and what her own experiment with writing had meant to her. The essay Axelson wrote that May begins with a candid statement of her bitter-sweet experience:

> My reflections on the writing-intensive course I taught seem to be full of 'I wish I had . . . .' But just as often I hear myself say, 'I'm glad that . . . .' In the first place, I wish I had learned to use writing-to-learn earlier in my teaching career. But I'm glad that I can use this technique for the few years I have left to teach.

Julein Axelson titled her essay "The Case of a Reluctant WAC Teacher." It was a title that many of Radford's teachers might have chosen for their own stories—including George Parish.

Despite his role as resident skeptic, despite the opposition he voiced publicly, despite the grave reservation he felt personally, George Parish began to explore the connections between writing and learning in his field of music theory. He began to experiment in the classroom, and shortly afterward he gave two public presentations of his new teaching practice to Radford faculty. He wrote up one of these as an essay—"Writing and Learning About Music" (1987)—which was printed and distributed for the whole staff. He found a book by a distinguished musicologist (somewhat ironically from his alma mater, Michigan) on the uses of writing in the teaching of music history and recommended it for inclusion in the Writing Across the Curriculum library. He advocated among his colleagues in the Mid-Atlantic College Music Society that space be given in their annual conference program to a session on writing and learning. When that idea was approved, he solicited participation from music teachers at other colleges and universities, and in April of 1987, he organized a panel of music teachers talking about writing.

In 1988 George Parish volunteered to teach his Second Year Theory class as a writing-intensive course. "The teaching of this course," Parish says, "was a kind of culmination of my WAC activity." In reflecting on his practices in this course, Parish reveals something of the transformation that his conception of teaching had undergone: "Initially, I viewed writing in class as taking time away from more fundamental activity—primarily my lectures and analyses. I began to realize, however, that I was in a position of giving perhaps brilliant lectures and classroom demonstrations that only a few students completely understood."

Parish began to include various informal writing activities in the class—summarizing lectures, formulating questions about the material, responding to musical works. He found that informal writing in class was an effective strategy, "saving rather than taking time, and certainly enhancing student learning." Parish says that the most important result of this kind of writing was "increased discussion by everyone in the class. In the past, class discussion tended to be dominated by the quick but often facile responses of a few 'bright' students. Now that everyone had written something down about the topic, more members of the class participated."

Parish found that the writing not only increased the amount of participation but improved the quality of participation as well. He offered this as an example of how the writing and the talk led to active learning in his class:

> This kind of writing led to the observation in the Haydn sonatina movement we were studying that the most difficult level of form to perceive was the phrase. This led in turn to more central questions regarding the matter: Why is the level of form difficult to perceive in this piece when usually it isn't a problem at all? What is the effect of this lack of clarity? And, of course, centrally, why did Haydn do it? In short, we moved from an agreed upon fact (that itself might not have been revealed as clearly without the writing) to central

questions of compositional process. ("Writing and Learning Music Theory," 1988)

George Parish found that he, too, was a learner in this experimental course; he learned something new about his role in the classroom, about how students learn, and even about music. "I've found," says Parish, "I can give up some control without losing my authority and also shift responsibility to the students where it really belongs anyway." With a certain amount of pride, he points to a comment made by one of his students on the course evaluation form: "I learned something about my own musical interests in the course of working on the term paper. Thanks!"

"Note," says Parish, "that the student did not say she learned from the paper; rather she learned 'in the course of working on the paper.' In other words, the process of writing was the key, not necessarily the product."

In describing one classroom activity intended to help students learn about the levels of tonal motion through the construction of reductive charts, Parish reveals that he, too, learned a new way of hearing a particular piece of music. "I had students write their reactions to various reductive charts and in one instance I gave them two alternative readings and asked them to justify which was correct. I actually had in mind that they would select chart one; however, at least some of those who selected chart two gave strong enough justification to show me that in fact it was not an absolutely incorrect rendering of the work at all; rather, in some particulars at least, it was another way to hear the piece."

George Parish has changed the way he teaches and his conception of teaching. He has undergone what he himself called "a revolution in teaching." Through his participation in the Writing Across the Curriculum program, George Parish, like Julein Axelson, Richard Straw, Karma Castleberry, Kim Kipling, Moira Baker, and dozens of their colleagues, has come to see that, as Nancy Martin puts it, "the word for teaching is learning."

Chapter Six

Students Writing
and Learning

When she applied for admission to Radford University in the spring of 1985, Mary Schultz was thinking more about the freedom of being away from home than about the educational quality of the institution she was about to enter, more about the social life that awaited her than about the academic challenges she would face. She had perused the literature sent out by the admissions office articulating Radford's primary commitment to teaching and student learning and announcing the university's emphasis on writing throughout the curriculum, but these institutional features were not foremost on her mind. Seventeen years old and in her final months of high school in Fairfax County, Virginia, Schultz was uncertain about her academic goals and undecided on her major field of study. In many ways, she was typical of Radford's incoming freshmen—over a quarter of them come from suburban areas of Northern Virginia, many from Fairfax County; ninety percent are 17 or 18 years old; one third have yet to decide on an academic major.

Thinking back on her reasons for choosing Radford University, Mary Schultz gives the following candid account:

> The first time I ever came to R.U. was Parents' Weekend in 1984. My brother Tim was here and we came down to visit. He lived on 5th floor Muse and he had made a lot of friends. . . . I had never seen Tim relate with people so well. I remember there was a kind of social gathering in the party room in Heth. All the guys and their parents were there. . . . . I was really overwhelmed with how nice Tim was being. . . . . I was only half joking when I said that if anyplace can turn Tim into a nice guy, it must be one hell of a place.

I ended up saying that a lot when people asked me why I came to
Radford. I suppose it was the attention I got from everyone here that
was really attractive . . . . A big part of why I came here was because
I kind of already felt established, thanks to Tim . . . . So . . . the
attention, the change in Tim's attitude, and the popularity of Radford as a college in my high school all played significant parts.

Continuing her musings, Schultz added a few more reasons to her
list. She liked the small size of the school. (Enrollments were under
7,000 at that time.) She was attracted by the appearance of the
campus and the surrounding countryside. She enjoyed what she calls
the "unpretentious feel" of the Radford community.

As personal as Schultz's reasons were for choosing Radford, they
are not unlike the reasons cited by many students. The week before
graduation in 1989, several of her classmates were interviewed for
Campus Currents, the faculty/staff newsletter issued by the Public
Information Office; each was asked to comment on what drew him
or her to Radford. Rosemary Oakes, a statistics major from Martinsville in southern Virginia, said she was drawn to Radford by its
friendly atmosphere and the personalized attention she received
when she visited the campus. Oakes's career goals involved working
with numbers, but she didn't want to be treated like one: "I wanted
to go where I was a name, not a number." David Pine, a marketing
major from Woodbridge in northern Virginia, said his decision to
attend Radford was not difficult—his sister is an alumna and besides,
he added, "Once I came down here I was sold on it. I like the
location." Linda Wallace, from the small town of Rocky Mount,
reported that she is the fifth person in her family to attend Radford.
And Lynn Munari of Lexington, Kentucky, about to become a second
generation Radford graduate, said her mother had urged her to apply
to Radford but her decision came when she toured a number of
prospective colleges. "I was immediately struck by the beauty of the
Radford campus," she recalled.

Even Radford's most academically oriented new students say that
such factors as the attractiveness of the campus and the friendliness
of the students, faculty, and staff were crucial in their decision to
enroll. Recipient of a Freshman Scholarship Award in 1987, Martin
Matulia from Frederick, Maryland, had never heard of Radford University until he unexpectedly received a packet of information in the
mail during the summer of 1986. He says the impression he got of
Radford from the literature made him eager to apply. Active in high
school athletics, editor of his school's newspaper, president-elect of
his senior class, Matulia was looking for a school large enough to
provide diverse extra-curricular activities but small enough to provide a personalized education. Radford seemed to fit the bill. But it

was not until he and his parents visited Radford in the autumn of his senior year that he was sold on the university. "The campus looked so good," says Matulia, "I fell in love with it."

Lori Scott, another merit scholarship recipient, says her decision to attend Radford was influenced by her brother Kevin, a former Radford student. "Kevin liked it here, and what he told me about the university made it appealing to me." Like many graduates of Christiansburg High School, just ten miles from Radford, Lori Scott says Radford was her first choice. Its location and its size were important to her. "I like the fact that everybody seems to know everyone else."

There are, of course, many other reasons why students choose Radford. The relatively modest cost of tuition is often cited—by both students and their parents. Some students mention the range of academic programs available; others refer to the reputation of specific departments and faculty members. A few frankly declare that Radford's "party scene" was one of the factors in their decision to attend the university.

In *College: The Undergraduate Experience in America,* Ernest Boyer reports the results of a nationwide survey of college-bound high school students conducted by the Carnegie Foundation for the Advancement of Teaching. The results suggest that the reasons offered by Radford students for selecting their college are not unusual. For nearly seventy-five percent of college-bound seniors, family and high school friends were cited as exerting the greatest influence in selecting a college (New York: Harper, 1987, 19). The survey found that in choosing a college students were more interested in "student activities and campus life" than in "strengths and weaknesses of faculty." They were more concerned about "costs of tuition, fees, books" than about "academic programs being offered" (21). And twelve percent of those surveyed said that a "very important" reason for going to college was "to have a few more years of fun" (12).

Boyer reports that the majority of college-bound high school students visit at least one campus before making their choice, and, when asked what influenced them most in their final decision, half of those surveyed mentioned "the friendliness of students we met." Boyer goes further: "But it was the buildings, the trees, the walkways, the well-kept lawns—that overwhelmingly won out. The appearance of the campus is, by far, the most influential characteristic during campus visits" (17). Reviewing the survey data and interviewing students on campuses across the country, Boyer says that he "gained the distinct impression that when it comes to recruiting students, the director of buildings and grounds may be more important than the academic dean" (17).

Most Radford students—whether they were attracted to the university by the look of its campus, by its size and location, by the range and quality of its academic programs, or by its reputed "party scene"—report that the collegial atmosphere and personal attention promised in the recruitment literature and demonstrated at Quest continue throughout their years at Radford. A survey conducted in 1988 by the Office of Student Assessment Programs found that the two most frequently cited causes of satisfaction with the university among that year's graduates were "friendships between faculty and students" and "helpful/caring faculty." Another survey conducted that year, this one with students who withdrew from Radford between 1987 and 1988, suggests a similar experience: "helpful instructors" and "teacher/student relationships" were named the leading sources of satisfaction during these students' time at Radford.

Mary Schultz says that many of the faculty at Radford made her feel more like a colleague than a "receptacle of information," and many "seemed to make a real personal investment in my progress and achievement." She mentions Jim Unnever, professor of sociology:

> I never took his classes, but my roommate and my brother both had him and they invited me to sit in. I ended up attending his class for the rest of the semester . . . partly because he was so passionate about what he was teaching. He seemed interested in each one of the students and incorporated student input into the class. Everyone was involved. He got me involved in the Progressive Student Alliance—a student organization for which he was faculty advisor. My involvement in that organization and my association with him gave me a real self-confidence.

And she mentions several others:

> Moira, Scott, Louis, Norman, Justin—I even call them by their first names . . . just sheds light on the kind of education I've gained— informal, and comfortable—which adds up to encouraging and supportive to me. Builds confidence. There's a respect here, an impressiveness of teachers that makes me feel special being able to address them on friendly familiar terms.

Tony Philpott, too, recalls the importance of personal relationships with faculty in shaping his college experience, in giving him self-confidence, identity. Born and raised in rural southern Virginia, the first member of his family to attend college, a black student entering a school where more than ninety percent of his classmates would be white—Philpott knew he would face many challenges, both academic and social, when he left home for college as a shy seventeen-year-old. Asked about his memories of Radford two years after his graduation, Philpott, without hesitation, offers the following anecdote:

> Radford is a place of change. This may sound silly, but there is something about my Radford experience that I'll never forget, that I *can't* forget. It's personal. My very first class was with Warren Self and on the first day he was reading the roll and when he called out my name he looked up and asked "Are you Anthony or Tony?" For my entire life I had been "Anthony." But at that moment I said "Tony." And I have been Tony ever since.

Tony Philpott had more stories to tell. In the summer between his freshman and sophomore years, he was at home in Martinsville working at a pharmacy to earn money for his college tuition. The previous spring he had applied for a work/study position and, though he was registered as a journalism major, he had requested a job with the English department. One evening he received a phone call; it was Warren Self. "I couldn't believe it," Philpott says, "a professor calling me—at home. He asked if I would be interested in a work/study position with Writing Across the Curriculum. I had never heard of WAC, but I said 'yes.' "

That "yes," Philpott now says, was fateful. Throughout his sophomore, junior, and senior years he worked for the program— typing copy for the newsletter, running errands, arranging meeting rooms, ordering books for the WAC library, attending panel discussions, engaging in dialogue with faculty about the value and uses of writing in learning. In the autumn of his senior year, Philpott was invited to participate in a weekend workshop at Pipestem State Park. Again he said yes. His account of that weekend and what the experience meant to him personally and academically was published in the program newsletter. He titled his essay "A New Perspective."

> One never quite knows what he's getting into when he says "yes" to a Writing Across the Curriculum coordinator. Recently I said "yes" to Coreen Mett when she asked me to attend a weekend retreat with twenty faculty members. . . . I soon found out how our educators behave when put together outside of a classroom setting. Of all the talking that teachers do in class, one would think that, when given the opportunity, they would do less. That was not the case. . . . Many times the discussions turned into debates about what is a better way of teaching writing as a learning tool. Or when there was a discussion of a certain author's writing, the atmosphere became tense with disagreements over the author's statements. . . .
>
> I was to write about my first WAC retreat. Instead I wanted to write about a group that stimulated my desire to encourage my peers to write more. The retreat proved that writing is a very important part of learning and that there are many faculty members who want

their students to recognize the importance of it. (*Writing & Learning* 7.4 [1989]:3)

Philpott's involvement in the work of Writing Across the Curriculum not only colored his memories of Radford, it helped shape the direction and activities of the program. One result of his participation in the faculty workshop is anticipated in Coreen Mett's report on that weekend. "We all came away wishing we had classes full of students like Tony," wrote Mett, "and more importantly, that we had the opportunity to learn with our students in this kind of intimate partnership."

The following year ten students were invited to participate in the autumn weekend workshop at Pipestem, and another group of students attended in the spring. And, like Tony Philpott and Coreen Mett, both students and faculty found the collaborative exploration of writing and teaching and learning both surprising and rewarding. One faculty participant commented, "The weekend has provided further insight for me into the processes needed to link students and teachers to a mutual goal—learning. Sharing thoughts and concerns from both sides of the lectern helps build the environment for enthusiasm and motivation about the shared task of learning." Another wrote that her "excitement has come from the dialogue between student and faculty." A student participant expressed his surprise this way: "I have found a new dimension of higher education, that is, learning—not studying to memorize but developing the hunger for knowledge. And a new dimension of 'teacher' has been exposed to me. You guys are fantastic individuals, willing to learn new and more positive ways to share with us."

At the same time that students and faculty were writing and talking together at Pipestem, another group of students—eighteen business and organizational psychology majors—were participating in a special weekend writing workshop at Doe Run Lodge on the Blue Ridge Parkway. These students had just returned from a three-day field seminar at the national headquarters of the Communications Workers of America (CWA) in Washington D.C. The extracurricular seminar, funded in 1989 by CWA as part of its Labor Education Program for future managers, had given these students an opportunity to meet and talk with union officials, to observe the process of labor-management negotiations, to learn first-hand about the workings of a labor union. At Doe Run, they talked and wrote and reflected on their experience. Their final papers were subsequently photocopied, bound, and distributed to all participants.

More recently, a weekend writing workshop was conducted for graduate students engaged in thesis work. Eleven master's candidates in different disciplines traveled to the Peaks of Otter to spend a weekend discussing issues and problems with their writing. They drafted sections of their theses, talked with their peers, revised, consulted with faculty advisors, and revised again. In his evaluation of the workshop, Dean Crane, a graduate student in the department of recreation and leisure services, wrote this about the off-campus writing experience:

> The weekend retreat helped my writing and thinking about the whole subject of the thesis tremendously. The team meetings gave me a chance to hear how others were doing and how they overcame their problems. Now that I have learned some of these helpful hints, it will make this journey easier for me. . . . I would recommend this to anyone who is doing a thesis.

Though she never attended an off-campus weekend workshop, Mary Hart found the program's ideas and collaborative practices valuable to her. In May of 1988, she joined a group of faculty meeting at Radford to talk and write about the experimental writing-intensive courses they had taught that year. Hart had double-majored in mathematics and statistics and had enrolled in Professor Coreen Mett's advanced statistics course called Operations Research. Together, Mett and Hart wrote essays about the course—Mett from the point of view of the professor who had designed and planned the course, Hart from the point of view of a student taking an advanced statistics class.

To emphasize the surprising quality of her experience in Operations Research, Hart entitled her essay "Not Just Another Class." The course's value to her was underlined not only by her essay but by her willingness to participate in the workshop at all. The previous Saturday morning, along with the other 1,250 students in her class, she had graduated on the lawn in front of McConnell Library. Monday morning, she was upstairs in Heth Hall, meeting with twenty faculty and preparing to spend the first week of her post-graduate life writing and talking with teachers.

When asked why she was willing to remain to do still more work, she says she never thought about it like that. "I felt really honored to have been asked. I never had to talk myself into it. Dr. Mett thought I had some insight, something she could use to help other people. That was pretty important to me."

Each morning of the workshop began with a buffet breakfast for all the participants; each afternoon small groups of four met to read and discuss the drafts of their developing papers. Mett and Hart wrote independent papers and participated in different writing groups. But in the middle of the day, they both worked in Reed Hall, the old science and mathematics building where Mett has her third-floor office. At different computers, they recollected their different experiences of the course. Then they stopped to read to one another and to talk.

About Hart's never imagining that there would be writing in a statistics course, for example, about her initial intimidation in Mett's class. In her account of the course, Hart explains: "It was the first time I had been scared when I looked at a syllabus." And about that syllabus, she says:

> Our grade was to be based on not only homework assignments and three in-class exams, which would come from our book and class notes, but also informal journal writings and a formal project to be written and presented orally. We were going to have to write in this class and be graded on it too! This was a new twist indeed.

Mett and Hart also talked together about the teacher's perspective. About Mett's attempts to get students to formulate new problems of their own, about sharing her own writing with them only to have them point out its flaws, about the mixed messages she gave them concerning the intended audience of some of their writing. The course was an experiment for Mett, and her collaboration with Hart was unprecedented. "I didn't know if it would be successful," she now says. "I didn't know where [our decision to write separate papers] would take us. But Mary became her own boss; her paper was her paper." And that meant that in their talk, Mett could discover things about the course she had not known—for example, the way the informal writing assigned in this unconventional mathematics course became the students' own.

"They were struggling with how to get started," she now explains, retelling an anecdote that Hart told her in her office:

> They sat around Jim Campbell's kitchen table [Campbell was another student in the course], struggling with how to get started and they finally decided let's each freewrite for a few minutes. . . . And that to me . . . gosh, all these things that we'd been doing in class that I thought were experimental and maybe helpful . . . they must have believed in. . . . It was a wonderful thing to find out.

The benefit of their work together did not stop there. Mett and Hart finished their papers for the Writing Across the Curriculum program. Then they turned them into a presentation for the Mid-Atlantic Conference of Teachers of Mathematics. And when a family emergency prevented Mett from attending the conference, Hart agreed to make the presentation alone. They subsequently revised and submitted their papers for publication in *Using Writing to Teach Mathematics* (1990). "I never pictured that," Hart now says; "I never dreamed of it. That's my name down there. I had something to say that somebody wanted to read."

Since the first writing-intensive courses were offered in 1986, they have become a central feature of Radford's Writing Across the Curriculum program. Some eighty such courses—ranging across the disciplines from accounting, biology, and computer science to recreation and sociology—have been offered. Close to 2,000 Radford students have been enrolled in them. On their course evaluation forms, many of these students have reported that they found the writing-intensive experience unexpectedly rewarding.

Some have said that the frequent informal writing—journals, logs, freewriting—and their teacher's response to this writing generate a sense of personal dialogue and intimacy with their professor. A student in Karma Castleberry's nursing class, for example, wrote: "I like the journal writing because it provided an opportunity to express my feelings about the course, frustrations, and areas I needed clarification in. . . . I could have contact with my professor and speak honestly." One of Grace Edwards's students commented: "The weekly journals were helpful to me. I could ask questions of Dr. Edwards, questions I would not or could not ask in class. . . . I enjoyed the comments that came back to me in the journal and felt that someone was really on the other end of the line."

Other students have reported that the sharing of their writing with their classmates produces a feeling of community in the classroom. "Writing all those short papers and reading them in class was great," said a student in a senior-level philosophy class, "because lots of different views and voices could be heard. We were all learning from each other. It felt like a team."

Still other students have commented that writing-intensive courses enhance their comprehension and retention of the subject matter. Some have reported that the use of writing changed their understanding of how they learn and what it means to learn. A student in Richard Straw's history class, for example, wrote: "I learned that just taking notes and studying for a test is not learning; it is memorizing. Writing on a topic is thinking and learning about the topic." One of this student's classmates offered a detailed account of the many benefits he had gained from this writing-intensive class:

> Writing so much helped me to work on looking past the obvious themes and ideas to something deeper. . . . Not only did I learn to express myself and my opinions better, I learned how to listen to others. . . . I liked the writings because they were challenging and I really got to know my fellow students better. . . . I think I am improving in my analysis skills thanks to this course. . . . What was most valuable in helping me write better was the exchange of

concepts, ideas, and opinions held by the members/teacher of the class. They helped me to stay away from the narrow-minded side of myself and helped me to see things in a different light.

While some students find the writing-intensive experience rewarding, others are less enthused. Accounting major Ken Hartwick enrolled in a business calculus class in which daily journals were required. At a subsequent faculty-student panel discussion, Hartwick expressed his views—and, he suggested, the views of many other students—about such writing assignments. While acknowledging the benefits of journal writing in terms of individual contact with his teacher, a clearer sense of his progress in the course, and increased retention of the material, Hartwick candidly declared that he would not have done this writing if he had not received credit for it. (In this class the journals counted for eight percent of the course grade.) Furthermore, he insisted that he would not continue to use journals—despite their benefits—unless he was required to do so and was given sufficient credit toward the final course grade.

In their anonymous end-of-the-semester evaluations, some students in writing-intensive courses express anger and frustration. It isn't fair, they say, to be required to do so much work and not even have this extra labor reflected on their transcripts. The freewriting, the journals, the formal and informal papers, some comment, are mere "busy work," a "tedious chore," and a "waste of time." Other students simply withdraw from the class after looking at the syllabus. Mary Schultz did not withdraw, but she did rebel.

It was the spring semester of her junior year. Having completed her 51-hour general education requirement, Schultz was eager to pursue her emerging intellectual interests—political philosophy, social theory, literary theory. She registered for fifteen hours that semester, an average load for a full-time student. Seventeenth-Century Literature, Advanced Fiction Writing, Principles of Literary Criticism, Marxism, Social Change—all required substantial amounts of writing. Schultz was caught by surprise: "I knew, of course, I would be doing a good bit of writing for Advanced Fiction . . . and Seventeenth Century Literature would require some writing, but . . . I didn't expect to do much writing in Social Change or Marxism. . . . My previous political science classes and sociology classes had been straight lecture. Not this time."

As it happened, the Marxism class was taught by Craig Waggaman that semester and was one of the writing-intensive courses sponsored by the Writing Across the Curriculum program. Seventeenth-Century Literature was taught by Moira Baker with writing-intensive methods she had developed the previous spring. Tom

Shannon was teaching the Social Change class and, though he had not designated it as writing-intensive, he had been influenced by the ideas and practices of the Writing Across the Curriculum program.

Schultz found herself immersed in writing: writing in response to reading assignments, writing in response to class discussions, writing in response to class presentations, writing essay exams and term papers. She quickly saw what this would mean for her reading. "No longer could I skim over the reading material just enough to understand class lectures. I had to engage myself with the texts. I had to immerse myself deep enough in the *Communist Manifesto* to be able to *write* about it. . . . I began to question and investigate more aggressively than I ever had before . . . and writing became a tool for me in a new way." Schultz now says, "I didn't learn all the answers to my questions, but I did learn something important. I became convinced that semester that writing is a fundamental and essential part of learning, not only about class material, but about oneself as well."

As valuable as this discovery seems to Schultz now, at the time her response was very different. She experienced that semester as a time of personal and intellectual crisis.

"Nothing I had ever done had demanded so much effort," says Schultz. She began to have doubts about herself and her ability to meet the challenge of those courses. She felt frustrated, victimized. And she rebelled. "Determined to fight the establishment which was responsible for my academic demise, I vowed to overcome the oppression and exploitation."

Schultz began to write in her class journals about how unfairly treated, how betrayed, she felt. She questioned the authority of institutional policies, the legitimacy of course requirements, the validity of classroom procedures. "Why wasn't I told about this writing-intensive stuff?" she demanded to know. "How come nobody warned me?" "We students," she protested, "shouldn't be subject to such abuse. We shouldn't be victims of such an imposition as writing-intensive courses. What is the Writing Across the Curriculum thing, anyway?"

Posed bluntly, Mary Schultz's question elicits diverse responses from Radford students. Many claim never to have heard of Writing Across the Curriculum. Others say they have heard the name but have no idea what the program is about. Some speculate. "I'm not sure," says Shannon Feagans, now a graduate student at Radford, "but I imagine it's to get people to be better writers." Another, Kim Spradlin, a sociology major, says she has heard it mentioned in several of her classes. "But I really don't know anything specific about the program. I know it exists, and to my understanding, it's a program that was started to get students more involved with writing to aid in all areas of their education." John Spraker, a former Writing Center tutor, comments, "It's like an organized thing . . . there is a core of professors who are WAC profs." Writing Across the Curriculum, Spraker says, is a program designed to offer faculty an opportunity to "talk about things related to their teaching."

Three years before Mary Schultz had, in exasperation, raised the question, "What is the Writing Across the Curriculum thing, anyway?" Rhonda Catron had innocently posed that question to one of the program coordinators. Catron, then a sophomore English major, had just received a phone call asking if she would be interested in the first work/study position allocated to Writing Across the Curriculum. "What is it?" she asked.

Catron was informed that the Writing Across the Curriculum program was an attempt to promote writing in all classes, not just in English classes. She was skeptical: "I must admit I had some doubts. Throughout my education I had written numerous papers, but the majority had been for English courses. The idea of writing in math or science just didn't seem relevant, but despite my reservations, I decided to accept the job."

For two and a half years, Catron served as a program assistant—at first alone, then with Tony Philpott. In the course of these years she witnessed the growth of the program and its growing effects on Radford faculty and students—especially on herself and her understanding of the role of writing in learning.

In April of 1987, her final month as a program assistant, and as an undergraduate, Rhonda Catron wrote an autobiographical article—"Growing with WAC"—for the program newsletter. It was her answer to the question she had raised more than two years earlier.

As I typed articles for the newsletter and information about panel discussions and workshops, I became increasingly interested in understanding what WAC was really all about. I started attending panel discussions sponsored by WAC and was fascinated by the kinds of issues that faculty were discussing. I listened as teachers— many who were skeptical just as I was—asked why they should consider using writing in their courses. They questioned if and how the use of writing would affect their classes. Many wanted to know how they were supposed to grade writing, arguing that writing was the responsibility of the English department.

I listened to these questions and the responses they received with interest. I heard teachers who had begun using writing in their classes report that their students seemed to have a better understanding of course material. Some professors said that writing encouraged students to think more about a subject. I realized that even though WAC didn't have or claim to have all the answers, it did have some very valid points about writing and learning.

I started to think about my own writing and learning. I looked back over my years in school and recalled that I had often had a basic fear of writing. I had generally cringed when a teacher had given an essay test or writing assignment. However, I was surprised to realize that I remembered those classes much more vividly than the courses that had required little, if any, writing. . . .

As I continued to think about my own writing, I learned even more about WAC through research that I did for the program. When asked to compile a list of sources on the evaluation of writing, I had a chance to read several interesting articles as well as to get acquainted with the books that were being purchased for the WAC library. I had the opportunity to talk with faculty who attended WAC activities and soon realized that I really believed in the WAC program and the ideas it promotes.

Since then my belief in WAC has continued to grow stronger. I find that my own writing is very important to my learning process. I often use writing to help me understand course content even if writing is not required by the professor. I am encouraged by the increasing number of faculty who are expressing interest in WAC because it seems to indicate that both faculty and students are becoming more aware of the value of writing for learning. . . .

One of my own professors, who had not been using writing assignments in our course, recently attended the WAC workshop conducted by Toby Fulwiler. It was exciting to see her try some of the writing exercises from the workshop that same afternoon in our class. With that kind of enthusiasm, I think—and definitely hope— that WAC has found a permanent place at Radford. (*Writing & Learning* 5.6 [1987]:6)

Whether or not the dialogue on writing and learning will continue at Radford University, whether or not "WAC" as a "program" becomes a permanent feature of the institution, this much is certain: the effects of Writing Across the Curriculum on some students have been far-reaching. Its presence has, for some, contributed in unexpected ways to their sense of Radford as a personalized learning environment, an institution where community is valued and fostered. For others, the ideas and practices of Writing Across the Curriculum have enriched their academic experience in ways never imagined, enlarging their understanding of what writing can be and can do, transforming their very conception of learning. And for at least a few students—Rhonda Catron, for example, and Tony Philpott and Mary Hart—the effects of the Writing Across the Curriculum program have extended even beyond their Radford years to influence their career goals and professional lives. Just as involvement in Writing Across the Curriculum has provoked in some faculty a heightened commitment to their work in the classroom and shifted their focus from teaching to learning, so too—in unintended and unforeseen ways—it has stimulated in some students a desire to become teachers.

When Rhonda Catron graduated she knew she wanted to enter the teaching profession. And she has. After two years as a Graduate Teaching Fellow, Catron earned her master's degree, then taught for a year as an instructor in Radford's English department. She is now on the faculty at Wytheville Community College near her hometown of Galax in southwestern Virginia. A paper she presented at a recent conference of the Virginia Association of Teachers of English suggests something of the continuing effects of her experience with Writing Across the Curriculum: Catron titled her presentation "Journals—Learning Tools for Student Writers and Their Teachers."

Catron's former co-worker, Tony Philpott, graduated in 1989 with a degree in journalism and a concentration in public relations. He has held a number of jobs since then—as a store clerk, a journalist, a substitute teacher. "I've found myself drawn more and more to the classroom," said Philpott in a recent interview. During the 1990-91 school year, he served as a substitute at various schools in the Martinsville area, including his old high school, Laurel Park. "It's been an interesting experience," he reports. "My former teachers treat me as a colleague. We talk a lot." In the summer of 1991 Tony Philpott applied to Lynchburg College to pursue state certification as a high school English teacher.

Mary Hart is married now, the mother of two, working as an actuary in the sort of mathematical career she always imagined for herself as an undergraduate. But what she calls the "inner benefit" of her experience with Writing Across the Curriculum and her collaboration with Professor Mett is still going on. "I never thought I'd want to go to school every day for the rest of my life," she says over the phone, but now? "I'm thinking of going back to school, to go into teaching. I think I want to be a teacher."

Chapter Seven

Making a Community, Making a University

Lee Stewart is one of the current coordinators of Writing Across the Curriculum. A professor of recreation and leisure services, she specializes in therapeutic recreation. She has worked in a variety of clinical settings and taught at four colleges. The appeal of the program to her is the appeal of Radford University. "It's the people," she says. "That's the key in it. The community. That's why I'm at Radford."

The door of her office is always open. At state conferences for recreational therapists, she meets many former students who are now in the field, now making their own way in the profession. At graduation in 1988, students stood to cheer for her when she was awarded the university's outstanding teaching prize. Though she has published very little, she was promoted to Full Professor in 1991. In addition to Writing Across the Curriculum, she has helped to coordinate a university-wide environmental education program, and she is working to establish a community-action volunteer program for students in Radford and the surrounding counties.

She tells a story about the community that she thinks Writing Across the Curriculum is helping to foster at the university. One spring she found herself carrying on two protracted conversations. The first was with a student in one of her classes. "He was bright," she says, "rebellious. Wore a headband and mismatched socks. He had flunked out of the University of Wyoming, gone to community college, excelled, and then transferred into Radford." He took advantage of her open door. In class and out, he talked with her. "He loved to argue," she says. "He was always challenging, always asking 'why?' 'why?' "

The same semester, a second-year member of the faculty began to ask her for advice about teaching. "He wanted to be an excellent teacher," Stewart explains now. "He was teaching a writing-intensive course, experimenting with the uses of journals, trying to create open classroom discussion." But he was deeply frustrated. Over lunches and coffee in the student union, he told her about an unnamed student he couldn't reach. "The student was very verbal. His abilities were clear. But he was negative, unwilling to participate, and he simply chose not to do the journal, even though he would miss points and maybe flunk the class." What this new teacher hoped for from Stewart was the answer to what to do, but he settled for a semester of talk.

The next fall it happened that Stewart and Coreen Mett were coordinating the weekend writing workshop at Pipestem. Forty-eight faculty and students participated. At the first break in the workshop, the faculty member with whom Stewart had spent the spring semester talking approached her in dismay: "Oh, no! Not him! My nightmare!" And sure enough, though Stewart had never made the connection before, there they were, her rebel student and her faculty friend, sitting across the table from one another, trapped together for a weekend of talk about writing and teaching and learning.

Stewart's story is not a fairy-tale of breakthrough rapprochement. Still, she watched them all weekend. And they *did* talk, and it seems to her that they left that workshop with something of a better understanding of one another, having helped one another—in spite of their conflicted past—to think about teaching and learning. And she concludes that Radford's Writing Across the Curriculum is the "only" academic program she has ever seen that would make such a mutual experience possible, bringing this student and this teacher together to be what she calls "fellow learners."

It was Noel Eggleston, professor of history, who first remarked on the community effect of Writing Across the Curriculum. In the Young Hall parking lot, early the morning after the first Writing Across the Curriculum panel discussion in the fall of 1982, he said, "That was a good session last night; I enjoyed it. I think it was a first."

The panel had included a biologist, explaining how he asked students to study the scientific method by describing tests for his mother's chicken-soup cold remedy. The chairperson of the communications disorders department had explained how writing cases for hearing-disorder patients helps students become not only more professional but more accurate diagnosticians. A business law professor had argued that the precision required in essay tests parallels the precision required in oral arguments and legal briefs. An anthropologist had discussed the notion that "goodness" in writing may depend more on purpose and context than on some generic criteria for good writing. About twenty faculty attended, among them the dean of the College of Arts and Sciences, himself a historian. The presentations and discussion went on for an hour and a half.

The next morning, walking across the parking lot, Eggleston said, "Since I have been at Radford, there has never been—to my knowledge—an event for faculty from different departments to come together and talk about teaching." He qualified his comment with characteristic caution, but his personal reaction was unambiguous: "It was very good."

Eggleston was widely regarded as one of Radford's best teachers. A scholar of the Vietnam War, he also served as advisor to a sorority, as a member of the student judicial board, and as a faculty assistant in the Quest orientation program. He lectured in the Governor's School. In 1984, he won the annual faculty award for outstanding professorial service. In commenting on the first Writing Across the Curriculum panel discussion, he was taking nothing away from the participants. But his emphasis was less on what they said than on the fact that they had come together at all. The talk itself was what struck him, the purpose, the surprising connection it created among faculty.

Ordinarily, Radford University is like most other academic institutions, a structure of cells. Administration. Faculty. Students. Town. Gown. Biology. Nursing. Management. But sometimes people are enabled to meet and work and learn together. Four colleagues from different departments, for example, attend a University of Chicago conference on writing and learning across the curriculum—fly together, room together, eat together, run together along the shore of Lake Michigan, talk nonstop together—and come back to Radford with a different sense of their relationship to one another on the faculty. The program asks them to make a public presentation for their colleagues on what they learned, so they meet for lunch at Sal's restaurant and talk some more, planning, rehearsing what they should say. All their other university business is colored by this experience. Whether they serve together on the Honors Council or accept appointment to an accreditation self-study committee, their rapport is changed by their having traveled and talked and thought together on behalf of the program.

Larry Terry, a professor of management and a specialist in the history and management of labor unions, wanted students to have the opportunity to learn from union officials themselves. After participating in a Writing Across the Curriculum weekend workshop, he got talking with another workshop veteran, Rene Rosenbaum, an economics professor specializing in labor history. The two teachers decided to take students to Washington to meet officials at the national offices of the Communication Workers of America (CWA). To prepare for the trip, they asked Susan Kirby to help them organize and conduct a weekend workshop for nineteen students, focusing on reading and writing about what they later called "the structure, functions, and processes of unions in general and the CWA in particular."

The workshop was funded by Radford's Writing Across the Curriculum program. But when the CWA office in Washington saw the complexity of Terry, Rosenbaum, and Kirby's project—and its potential as an educational model for other union districts—it took over funding. Since then, two additional groups of students have been involved in similar labor education seminars, conducted by Kirby and Terry: a three-day trip to Washington, a weekend workshop for drafting papers, and a follow-up collection of essays, published informally and distributed to all the students. Kirby and Terry themselves have written about this series of projects; their article ("Toward a Better Understanding of Unions: An Education Program for Future Managers") has been published in the *Labor Studies Journal* (17.1 [1992]).

Sociologist Larry Hembroff was an active participant in the Writing Across the Curriculum program at Radford until he moved with his family to take a teaching and research position at Michigan State. While at Radford, he made a faculty presentation on writing in the social sciences, attended a weekend workshop, shared his writing in a writing group, traveled off-campus, wrote for the newsletter, and talked informally with other faculty inside and outside his department about writing and learning. He also engaged students in collaborative research into the attitudes and behavior of Radford undergraduates, research they were then expected to write up and present. Since moving to Michigan, he has found himself again and again talking with his new colleagues about writing across the curriculum and about the Radford program. What it seemed to stress for him, he now says, is something he found himself writing about at the first weekend workshop at Pipestem in 1984: cooperation, shared learning, the mutuality of a duet.

When he was a boy, Hembroff wrote, he took guitar lessons every Monday night from Fred LaLonde at the Atkinson Music Studio in Sault Ste. Marie. The boy's teacher would not merely listen and instruct; he wanted to play, too.

It wasn't the instructor watching and listening to the student play, waiting to point out each flaw, to pounce on each imperfection. It was Fred and Larry playing a song. A duet. We weren't expecting each other to be perfect, only to be trying to be better, to make the music better together. ("Still Practicing," 1984)

Lee Stewart traveled with Rosalyn Lester, a professor of fashion and chairperson of her department, to a week-long summer workshop for teachers at Bard College's Institute for Writing and Thinking. Stewart and Lester already were acquainted with each other, having met during a semester in which they both taught writing-intensive courses. But their week of workshop sessions, writing, and talk convinced them of something they had not anticipated. Not only did they want to apply the ideas they were learning in their own classrooms; they wanted to replicate their experience for local school teachers at home.

With the help of Warren Self, the Virginia State Department of Education, and the administration of the Radford City school system, Stewart and Lester prepared and conducted a workshop for Radford teachers the following summer. Eleven high-school and middle-school teachers enrolled. Biology, math, social studies, French, English—the participants taught many different subjects. Drawing on the Bard model of intensive reading and writing, Stewart and Lester led the group through a week-long examination of their individual curricula and teaching practices and helped them develop experimental approaches to the uses of writing in their classes for the coming academic year. Then, during that year, they met periodically with the participant teachers to discuss the progress of their ideas about their teaching.

One of the teachers, biologist Frank Taylor, says now that it was not only a very positive personal experience but "unique." It was the "only forum," he says, where he and his colleagues had ever gotten together to talk about teaching. "We have all these faculty meetings all the time, of course, but we never talk about education." The subject of the workshop—writing—was important and valuable to him. He has since used many of the techniques he learned and has devised others to use in his secondary science classes, graduate courses he teaches for science teachers through the University of Virginia, and consulting programs for the Virginia Museum of Natural History. "So it's had a big impact on me," Taylor says simply. But the most important thing he stresses about the workshop is its giving him an occasion to talk with his fellow teachers—"just to *be* with them, talking about teaching."

University-sponsored inservice workshops for local school divisions are not new, of course. But this one was conceived and implemented by two faculty who a short time earlier had known one another only slightly and had never worked together. They taught in different departments (neither of them English), in different undergraduate colleges at Radford. Neither of them had used much writing in her own teaching before becoming involved with the campus Writing Across the Curriculum program. And the workshop project required the fullest collaboration between them. What they taught their teacher-students had to be selected and shaped in concert, and the very principles upon which they worked—though they had both experienced the Bard workshop— had to be redefined together.

One result of this project is that both Lester and Stewart became coordinators of the program. Their cross-disciplinary collaboration off campus evolved into a continuing working relationship within the university as well. The program has promoted other collaborations, too. In the fall of 1987, then vice president for Student Affairs, Jim Hartman, attended a faculty weekend workshop. The writing he did then—and the writing and talk he observed his faculty colleagues doing—suggested to him that writing might play a more important role in extra-curricular student activities at Radford. Judicial deliberations, planning, Quest orientation training, conflict resolution— in a whole raft of different areas, Hartman saw the possible benefits of using writing to help students learn and act. It also occurred to him that writing could be used in civic affairs.

At the time, Hartman served on the Board of Directors of the Radford City Chamber of Commerce. He proposed that, in the board's annual day-long planning session, it use the kinds of writing exercises he had experienced during the weekend workshop. Together with the board's executive-director, Rosemary Middleton, Hartman asked Rich Murphy for help in organizing and conducting such a writing-based Chamber of Commerce meeting. Though it was a highly unusual approach for the merchants and professionals on Radford's board, all reported that it was a great success. Even if it had not been, however, the collaboration of Middleton, Hartman, and Murphy would itself have been valuable. From offices whose work practically never intersects, the vice president for Student Affairs and an English professor came together for a time to be colleagues, bringing the academic work of the university into the town.

Sometimes the working occasions structured by the Writing Across the Curriculum program connect participants more subtly— in thought, in imagination, in shared ideas. The reiterated message of the program is that faculty are trying all sorts of assignments and approaches to help their students learn better. When some faculty see or hear or read about such efforts to observe and improve teaching, it fosters in them a sense of common purpose. They belong to a faculty, they feel, where their own interest in and commitment to teaching are valued.

Karolyn Givens, for instance, conducted a research project of her own which connected her to her Radford colleagues. During her first faculty weekend workshop, Givens began to think about the uses of writing in teaching. A member of the faculty of the School of Nursing, Givens realized that the nursing curriculum was highly technical but that writing could help her students personalize it and thus make it more accessible both to memory and understanding. First with colleagues, Karma Castleberry and Marcella Griggs, then with faculty from other departments—Marty Turnauer from Health and Physical Education and Lee Stewart from Recreation and Leisure Services—Givens talked about the possibilities of assigning her students informal writing about the scientific and professional concepts in their textbooks.

Her earliest teaching experiments with such writing were so promising that she decided to study the process more systematically. For her doctoral research—in recent years, the Nursing School at Radford has been urging its teaching faculty to return to graduate school to acquire doctorates—Givens studied the writing of a number of her students. During her research and writing, she continued to teach and to participate in the Writing Across the Curriculum program. When she completed her dissertation, she conducted a seminar for Radford faculty on the purposes and findings of her research, completing a circle begun years before. At the seminar she led, she returned to the kind of program and the kind of faculty gathering (though with many new faces) where she had, herself, first gotten ideas that had radically influenced her teaching.

Sometimes the resonance of such connections extends even further. Parks Lanier, poet and professor of English, was asked during 1983 if he would make a brief panel presentation on writing about literature. He did, using as his text Jeff Daniel Marion's short poem "Tight Lines," a poem at once about fishing and writing ("First read the water, / then cast toward pockets, / the deep spaces between / the cold print of rocks . . ."). Later, Lanier revised his presentation for the first faculty collection, *Working Papers on Writing and Learning* (1983). Nancy Martin was so struck by Lanier's piece when she read it in preparation for her first visit to Radford University in 1984 that she asked especially to meet him. Lanier was struck in turn by Martin's presentation to the faculty. During it—when she gave all the participants an opportunity to write—he began a poem of his own, using a different metaphor for writing. In a recent poetry lesson at a neighboring high school, Lanier had asked students to generate metaphors for writing to parallel Marion's fishing. Lanier took one of those metaphors, credited the student whose idea it was, developed it into a poem of his own, and published it in the faculty newsletter to commemorate Nancy Martin's visit. The last lines of "The Weight-lifter" read: "Struggling, / He remembered the slogans and rules, / Came to know words have weight / And must be lifted higher than the lifter / If their dull iron is to be enlightened / By his strength" (*Writing & Learning* 3.4 [1985]: 2).

The connections between persons fostered by Writing Across the Curriculum may be much less public than this, however. Sometimes they may be so silent as to be virtually imperceptible, calling attention to themselves only by gesture. Jim Corbet, for example, a professor of mathematics, has participated in a number of program activities. But outside of those occasions he almost never sees his colleagues. Normally, he is absorbed by his teaching and his research. He is also a very private person, his words spare. In the spring of 1987, during a faculty workshop, he began to write a short story about his boyhood relationship with his father. He was unable to complete it in the short time the workshop provided. But one morning in the middle of November, 1988, Murphy—who had been one of the members of his writing group—received an envelope in the campus mail with Corbet's finished story. "A New Beginning" it was called, nine pages of sharply selected details of the day he watched his father expertly rope a bull for branding and cutting, the day his relationship with his father changed. "How I wish I could go back and relive those moments," he wrote. "I never told Dad how I felt." There was no note attached to the story, but Murphy knew that it was a gift.

Some faculty have participated in the program so regularly that their sense of connection to one another and to it is especially strong. They feel themselves identified with it. It has come to seem a group to them as well as a program, and their membership in it is one of its attractions for them. Richard Straw, for example, says that he considered himself privileged to participate. The other faculty in the program, he said, "were people that I had a lot of respect for as teachers. My participation in the program was something that I felt had brought me into contact with the best teachers at the school. I was just thrilled to be part of that group of people, people that came to the programs, came to the workshops, participated in writing exercises or participated in Writing Across the Curriculum on a lot of different levels." When he was asked to help plan the future development of the program and to serve on its Advisory Council, he says he was "especially happy to be thought of as a person who might be able to contribute."

One small indication of faculty satisfaction in being part of a group has been their insistence on using the acronym "WAC." In spite of its currency in the professional literature on writing across the curriculum, the early coordinators, Murphy and Self, tried indirectly to discourage its use. For years, they themselves avoided using it, either in their announcements and reports or in their talk. But the regular faculty participants in the program took it up anyway, and one reason—other than its efficiency—seems to have been the familiarity it expressed. The program was enough their own to permit their use of an acronym that to nonparticipants was obscure but to them carried the affection of a diminutive.

The program has thus fostered—by the way it has structured connections among faculty—a sense of community among its participants. One unintended consequence of this sense of community, however, is that it has come to seem, to some observers, clique-like. Though most of its activities are completely open and advertised to all faculty, those who elect to participate most often are seen by some as "insiders," and the program has come to seem exclusive. In fact, it is not. Faculty participation in the Writing Across the Curriculum program has been very fluid. Some people have attended one event and never come back. Some have spent years intensively involved in the program's activities, only to gradually withdraw and devote their energies to other projects. Some faculty have participated only infrequently in scheduled programs but have read the newsletter and listened to bits of colleague talk about writing in their classes and have been led by it to reflect anew on their teaching. Invitations to faculty to attend weekend workshops are sent to all regular faculty, and everyone new or old is offered the opportunity to go. Administrator and student invitations are selective, in keeping with the original emphasis of the program on faculty development. But all members of the faculty have been solicited and encouraged to participate in the Writing Across the Curriculum program, and those who have accepted the invitation in one form or another have realized its essential openness. Still, the impression of exclusivity is one that faculty most active in the program have deliberately sought to minimize and with only limited success.

One source of the tenacity of this impression is that it provides faculty who are ill-disposed toward the program (for whatever reason) with a plausible excuse: They do not participate because they are not "insiders." But the impression of exclusivity also results from the enthusiasm of the participants. Sometimes the spirit of the program's meetings, sometimes the buoyant feeling of the faculty, disarms even them. They say—with some embarrassment—that it reminds them of a religious revival. In a journal entry after the first Pipestem weekend workshop, biologist Chuck Kugler referred to the program as "The Pipestem Holiness Revisionary Church." Melinda

Wagner, an anthropologist specializing in rural American religious cultures, says that, for some faculty at least, participation in "WAC" is like a conversion experience. There's a fervor to it, a psychological jubilation, akin to that felt by members of a church in communion.

Most faculty involved in Radford's program would not use her terms, but many can recall specific moments of such exhilaration that her analogy does not seem too extreme. Faculty who did not know each other on Friday afternoon gather together for group pictures on Sunday. Teachers from different departments come together to read their writing to one another and are so moved by one of their colleagues' stories that they ask her to read it aloud to the whole group. Karma Castleberry's piece, for example, "Lasting Impressions," in which she recounts her experience as a nurse of meeting in a shrunken old patient the teacher she had been terrified of in first grade. (Before Castleberry had even finished revising the story, members of her writing group wanted the whole workshop to hear.) Particular workshops acquire the quality of myth—Pipestem I; Pipestem II; the snowbound April of 1986 at Mountain Lake; the writing-intensive course workshop in May of 1987; the 1990 weekend devoted to the study of opera and geology. Some of these moments were so intense for participants that the name of the place or the time has come to embody for them the whole complex experience of people, ideas, writing, and hope.

Faculty colleagues stopped by one of these enthusiasts with a glittering eye are apt to feel excluded from the program by virtue of their own sobriety. But they are also inclined to be patronizing or skeptical. "Besides making you feel good," they are inclined to ask, "what is the program doing?" During one weekend workshop, for example, Radford sociologist Nelda Pearson wanted help using writing geared to the specific content of her discipline. Instead she was asked to write a series of what she later called "exercises," which were mostly personal and informal and which frustrated her with their irrelevance to her professional concerns. One piece she wrote— about herself as a girl in a canoe on a lake with sunlight on her, in her—she dismissed as sentimental. Before reading it aloud to the larger group of her colleagues, she said, "Don't you dare applaud." When she read, they applauded anyway. The satisfaction felt by some faculty is deeply personal. One year the program's annual report to the president ended with a quotation from a newsletter article by Rita Riddle, professor of English: "I can't think of any activity that I've shared in at Radford University that has made me feel more alive as a teacher—and as a human being."

Such a personal testimonial alienates some Radford faculty, but for others it serves as one more statement of their common feeling of excitement and value in the work of the Writing Across the Curriculum program. Riddle's words bring together two essential elements of that work—teaching and community. Working together has created both common memories and shared aspirations. Lee Stewart says, "I like the people of WAC personally but that's because I respect them as professionals. They're committed to the same things. It has allowed us to know each other. People are friends." But the difference this has made for her is not merely personal. "I may not see someone I've worked with in the program for three months, but when I see him there is a connection, a concern, a caring. I know he cares about teaching. It has made us all better teachers. I am a better teacher now because of this program."

Even faculty who have a less affective response to the program value its talk. Noel Eggleston's observation the morning after the first panel discussion has been repeated again and again since: Like nothing else at Radford, this program brings faculty together to talk about teaching. J.D. Hansard, for example, explains that, before the program, there was never anything like this. What if he wanted to think about teaching? "I talked to myself," he says. In his experience, mathematicians almost never say anything to one another about teaching. So "this Writing Across the Curriculum thing appealed to me because it gave me a chance to think about and talk about the teaching process." It allowed him to slow down, to concentrate his attention on teaching, to think, for example, about how to teach quadratic equations. It gave him time, and insight. Listening to other people talk about learning, he says, made him realize what always came as a surprise—that "I could make my teaching better."

Hansard came to Radford in 1969, three years before Donald Dedmon. He has observed the whole history of Writing Across the Curriculum and the whole twenty-year transformation of Radford as an institution. When he tries to explain the effect of the program on the university, he says that his impression is that it created among at least some faculty "a kind of positive cohesion." And he too describes its contribution as unique. "It was almost the only thing of any kind," he says, "to create community across the culture."

Hansard also believes that it has affected the very character of the university. A "university" is not really an organization, he says, nor even a faculty disconnected from one another and representing a whole range of different viewpoints. Under normal circumstances, these disparate elements are brought together, if at all, only in the mind of the individual student. Writing Across the Curriculum at Radford, however, has allowed the faculty to be students again, to be learners themselves, and thus, according to Hansard, to embody in themselves "the spirit of a true university."

If his assessment is accurate, then the Radford faculty who have participated most fully in this program have felt what Nancy Martin and her colleagues in LATE must have felt in 1968, working together to understand the place of talk and writing in their pupils' learning. What was being made there was not only a writing-across-the-curriculum movement but a community. And only in the community of teachers working together could the movement itself be said to exist. For at least some faculty, Radford's program has created a community that embodies the hope they feel for the emerging character of the institution.

The night before Larry Hembroff moved away, for example, he sat in the dark on a colleague's front porch. The rental van was packed with furniture, his old house empty and clean. In the morning, he and his family would set off for Michigan. Hembroff had driven over to say good-bye, and to remember.

"This has been good," his voice said, disembodied. "To be part of this . . . working together to make a university."

Chapter Eight

Creating an Image, Creating a Culture

Like many other public colleges in America in the 1990s, Radford University is trying—under the influence of competing pressures—to define itself. Like many others, too, it is creating images of itself for the public. These are not the same processes, but inevitably they intertwine. What the institution is and wants to be influences its choice of images, and the images in turn—though intended for others—help to shape its own sense of itself.

For ten years, the Writing Across the Curriculum program has been part of this process. It has benefitted from the university's studied creation of an institutional image. It has suffered from the negative reaction to what some regard as mere public relations. And it has provided the university with a public sign of its academic character and purpose. This interaction is one essential element of the program's history at Radford: it has acquired institutional support because it serves the university's image-creating purposes; at the same time it has helped to create the academic culture toward which the institution is striving.

In the competition among institutions of higher learning for funding, in their efforts to cultivate donors, inform alumni, attract students, and interest the public, creating images is necessary. Radford University is, therefore, not unusual in attempting to craft carefully its public profile. But everyone agrees (though for different reasons) that image is especially important to Radford. Its own recent history makes at least some of the reasons for this preoccupation understandable.

When Donald Dedmon became president of Radford in 1972, it was a desperately troubled college. Whatever the causes had been, the institution was in serious decline. Internally, suspicion and hostility between faculty and administration had grown so keen that the governance of the college was practically paralyzed. Externally, the public perception of Radford had so deteriorated that, at a time when other Virginia colleges were experiencing enrollment increases, students were applying to Radford in ever decreasing numbers. The students themselves were disaffected. The college's strict concern with regulating their social lives alienated them from the administration and seemed anachronistically irrelevant to their education.

Dedmon arrived and, according to news accounts of the time, immediately provided symbolic evidence of change. Though his new job did not officially begin until July 1, he came in mid-spring. "Things are too slow. Always things are too slow," he told a reporter later. "I believe in the immediate. I want it done" (*Roanoke Times and World News*, 30 September 1984). He rejected plans for an elaborate ceremony to inaugurate him as president and recommended that the funds be used instead to establish two scholarships for students. He moved into one of the college dorms and ate his meals in the dining hall so that he could be available to students from 7:00 a.m. until 11:00 p.m. This, in an institution where informal extracurricular relations between students and faculty and administrators had been frowned upon and had grown increasingly rare. The former president, Charles Martin, had regarded walking across the campus lawns as a grave offense. Dedmon ordered the fences around the lawns removed. A month after he arrived, he surprised organizers by signing up for a twenty-mile, fund-raising walk for hunger and thus gave not only his endorsement but new excitement to an extracurricular student project. Less than a week after arriving, he delivered his first convocation address. One reporter described it as "a rip-roaring, turned on, informal gathering of the entire Radford clan. No one was disappointed. A dozen times he was stopped by applause. By any measure, [it] was an unqualified success" (*Richmond Times Dispatch*, 2 April 1972).

Dedmon signified in his own words and actions the new energy and optimism he hoped to see Radford begin to foster. "I work long hours," he told local reporters when he arrived. "I go a mile a minute. I'm an early riser and I like to really work at something. . . . I naturally rather hope that people around me will work, too." He wanted to put an end to the pervasive depression of the college: "You can't think negatively. You must think and act positively, and I'm going to do everything I can—and I'm just going to expect no less from anybody else" (*Roanoke Times and World News*, 21 March 1972). To students and faculty who had come to feel unimportant and alienated, he brought a refreshing message: "The business of a college is students and the principal concern of both the faculty and administration is, and always will be, the 'teaching transaction.' Radford College shall be unmistakably committed to teaching and learning" (*Grapurchat*, 30 March 1972). In November of 1972, Dedmon delivered a special convocation speech devoted to rebuilding the fractured community of the college:

> At Radford we dream not only of growth, change, and unshakable service to our students; we dream also of a climate of enjoyment, excitement and the enormous psychic reward born of love, respect, trust, and the professional and personal commitment of every person who claims membership in our academic community.

And his dream for Radford, he said, included a future for the institution as well—that it develop and implement "imaginative new programs and procedures sufficient to move this college into a position of innovative leadership in the Commonwealth."

It was image-building Dedmon was undertaking. He told reporters explicitly that that was what he was doing, though he also said he did not like the term (*Roanoke Times and World News*, 21 March 1972). Still, on more than one occasion since, he has described his role as president in precisely these terms. A college president should be projecting a positive image for the university, he has said: "You have to tell people in various ways what you are" (*Roanoke Times and World News*, 30 September 1984).

And the ways are various. They include, for example, the alumni magazine, *Radford*, established in 1979. Its first editor, Joan Lentczner, echoed Dedmon's words in describing the magazine's purpose. "Our mission," she said, "is to give a positive, accurate story of what the university is trying to do." With vigorous stories, on heavy paper, with fine-grained graphics and striking color photographs by university photographer, Jack Jeffers, the magazine tries three times a year to portray the best elements of the institution's life.

The university also distributes a handsomely printed monthly calendar of campus events, suggesting the richness of its academic and artistic offerings: lectures on law and the economy, classic and popular films, recitals, concerts, distinguished visitors, lecturers, musicians, writers reading from their work—Maya Angelou, Maxine Kumin, Elie Weisel, William Stafford, Doc Watson. Members of the academic community perform for each other as well. In the studio theater, student directors stage productions of short plays of their choice to small, packed houses. Religious Studies professor Russell

Gregory recently had a play of his own produced by the studio company. The music faculty and students regularly perform publicly: the university orchestra and band, for example, under the director-ship of Mark Camphouse; piano recitals by David Phillips; song recitals by David Castonguay. The Appalachian Events Committee, a group of faculty and students from different departments (English, History, Sociology, Anthropology, Music), arranges every year a series of programs meant to inform and delight the community with the heritage of arts and crafts of this region. One such event—the Appalachian Craft Festival—brings local artists to the main lawn of the campus to display their quilts, musical instruments, firearms, tools, and baskets, and to explain the history and heart of their craft.

The 1989 Annual Giving Report, prepared by the University Foundation, featured a major land gift to Radford. Donated by John Bowles, the 184-acre tract, four miles from campus, includes forest, meadowland, cliffs, and river. The land has been declared a conser-vancy by the university, and students and faculty are both at work there, mapping its terrain, studying its ecology, documenting its history in county records, examining and preparing to restore its buildings.

University publications also showcase the Flossie Martin Art Gallery, which was opened in 1987 thanks to a donation by a grateful alumna in honor of one of her teachers at Radford College. The gallery produces a variety of shows every year in a broad range of media, as well as its regular display of faculty and student work from the department of art. On the lawn outside the gallery, a new sculp-ture garden has been established—named for Corinna de la Burde, a Radford student and the daughter of a gallery benefactor. Brochures from the Admissions Office do not, in fact, exaggerate: "The school calendar is packed with dances, movies, speakers, dramatic produc-tions, top-name entertainers, art exhibitions plus many other cultural and social events."

Radford makes a concerted effort to tell the public what it is by the way it looks. Visitors to the campus are always struck by its beauty and cleanliness. Lawns, flower beds, windows, floors, class-rooms, public halls—the campus is in excellent repair. Students from other colleges are astonished by the condition of the dorms. The halls and stairwells are plain, but trash-free and absolutely without graffiti. Classrooms are made immaculate, every day. The gutters along the sidewalks around the campus are themselves scoured. Before eight o'clock every morning, maintenance crews with large cream-colored plastic garbage bags pick up the soda and beer cans, fastfood bags, and paper cups that lightly litter the university grounds. "Most people don't know we do that," says Bobby Nicholson, the assistant director of the physical plant. "But before people get up and get going in the morning, we want it looking good." (When someone tells him how lovely a campus it is, he takes it personally and smiles his thanks.) From April until October, the groundskeeping crew spends nearly half of every week behind push mowers and on lawn tractors, inching with whining weedeaters around every edge. The university landscape director plants and replants banks of annuals, shifting their colors to give the quads both brilliance and surprise.

The most striking visual symbol of Radford's vitality is the Dedmon Center sports complex, completed in 1987. Photographs of its pristine white fiberglass roof and olympic pool hang on the walls of the Board of Visitors' conference room. Nearly every publication distributed by the Admissions Office to prospective students and their parents highlights the Center. At the end of the broad avenue that curves down toward the New River from Norwood Street, it arches up out of a green berm of lawn, starkly white, futuristic. Inside and out, like all the buildings and grounds at Radford, it is kept scrupulously clean, on display, a symbol of both the achievement and aspiration of the institution.

It is in the context of this pattern of image-building that the Writing Across the Curriculum program received the enthusiastic support of the university administration. In the first months of the program, the *Radford* magazine decided to run a major story on it. Editor Lentczner says that by November of 1982, her office had already received a clear message from the president's office that this program was a top priority item. The message was clear also in the informal university relations group of which Lentczner was a member. When this group—the Executive Assistant to the President, the Director of Development, the Director of Alumni Affairs, the Public Information Officer, the Athletic Director, and Lentczner, the Director of Publications and News—met late in 1982, it was clear that the university was going to commit itself to articulating and communicating the work of the Writing Across the Curriculum program.

In faculty convocations, in recruitment speeches to prospective students and their parents, in funding presentations before the state legislature in Richmond, in private meetings with state government officials, in letters to benefactors, in foundation annual reports, and in as many other ways as he has been able to think of, Donald Dedmon has highlighted the Writing Across the Curriculum program. It is a sign of what, when he first came to Radford, he called the institution's "unmistakable commitment to teaching and learning."

The very caution Dedmon himself early voiced about the term "image-building" is felt by others. Images run the risk of seeming specious, image-makers insincere. Like advertisers. But it is *to* advertising that Dedmon has turned to explain Radford's presentation of itself to the public. In his 1984 convocation speech to faculty, Dedmon used the term coined by Al Ries and Jack Trout in *Positioning: The Battle for Your Mind* (New York: McGraw-Hill, 1981). Radford has to "position" itself in the mind of the public, he said, and it has done so successfully:

> We have positioned ourselves well in the minds of a lot of people. We are not alone in seeing this institution for what it is; so do others in considerable numbers—and they like what they see: a comprehensive, co-educational, residential, mid-sized institution which emphasizes teaching. The campus is viewed as a personalized one. Students anticipate—quite accurately—that they will be respected as individuals, that they will have a chance to know some of their professors, and that they will have a chance to be a participant in, rather than be a casual observer of, the academic community. . . . We have communicated well our desire to be an excellent, comprehensive university without becoming huge in order to do so. . . . All these descriptions may sound like so many lines of jargon to you, but I can assure that they add up to an image of Radford University that is at once accurate, extraordinarily appealing, and unique. Radford has successfully positioned itself in the minds of the publics we serve.

In the midst of this confident description, Dedmon indirectly admitted how ambiguous a process "positioning" is. Addressing the faculty, he declared, on the one hand, that they see Radford for what it is. But then he paused to assure his audience that he was speaking accurately. Why should such reassurance have been necessary if the very people to whom he was speaking were those who know the institution and whose knowledge of it he was invoking? Why should the speech itself have been necessary if the image of Radford is already "extraordinarily appealing"? In fact, Dedmon's words themselves here are part of the positioning process. They are not merely a description of Radford, but an assertion of its aspiration. Description and assertion blur, desire becomes fact; the image of what the university aspires toward becomes the image of what it is.

The question of what Radford *is* has been the fundamental institutional question since Dedmon first came to the university. The future was open, he told his first audiences, and it was Radford's job to find its own niche. "Who are we," he asked, "and what is our reason for being?" (*Roanoke Times and World News*, 21 March 1972). These are still open questions. In spite of Dedmon's insistently positive portrait of the university (perhaps partly because of it), some observers are skeptical. They claim that Radford's images are illusory and that its character as an academic institution is deeply uncertain.

All college faculties include some members who seem to take delight in disparaging administrative leadership or student ability and performance. But at Radford, faculty criticism of this sort seems part of a larger institutional puzzle. Radford must create "an environment where excellence is 'in,' " says one faculty member in a recent survey of faculty attitudes. The same idea is echoed by another who criticizes the university for an academic calendar and social life that have the effect of "de-emphasizing academics."

Even Quest, the aptly named university orientation program, comes in for such criticism. As helpful a program as it is for introducing new students and their parents to the school, for making them feel welcome, and for fostering a positive attitude in them at the start of their careers at Radford, some observers worry that the underlying Quest message is not academic enough. Its very friendliness and individual attention—like the humor of the president's welcoming speech—seem to some misleading. Though an important part of the Quest program involves orienting students to the university's academic requirements and helping them register for their first semester of classes, little time is devoted to academic presentations. No lectures are offered by faculty on subjects of general interest; the schedule includes no artistic exhibitions or performances by faculty or students. As a result, the Quest orientation confirms the president's emphasis on Radford's personal quality without confirming his emphasis on its primary purpose: teaching and learning. And this apparent disjunction of purposes reinforces the view—among faculty, students, and the public at large—that Radford is a university with a vibrant social, but only modest academic, life.

Perhaps the greatest challenge facing Radford in defining itself as a university is to find ways to integrate the different elements of its cultural life. Faculty have met frequently in recent years to discuss ways to improve what they are calling the "academic environment" at Radford. After several years of discussion and bureaucratic review, some changes have recently been implemented that faculty hope will underscore the academic purpose of Radford. Among the changes are these: students are no longer able to drop courses late in a semester without penalty; the total number of course withdrawals an undergraduate is permitted in his or her program has been sharply reduced; mid-semester grades are now issued for all freshmen; and the library staff has been urged to consider expanding its hours of operation.

Even to some faculty most concerned about the university's academic environment, however, these changes seem unlikely to have a discernible impact. They are expected to have little effect on what some faculty consider the general lack of preparation, initiative, or commitment of Radford undergraduates or their apathy or distraction. Attitude surveys of faculty, administrators, and students—some conducted by Steve Culver of the Office of Student Assessment Programs; some by Betsy Little, the Coordinator of University Planning—all point toward the same general profile. Radford students are generally interested in academic success, but they are not very clear about their academic direction. They "need to put more serious effort into their studies," one faculty member wrote; and another stated that they need more "motivation to do the best possible college work."

One characterization of Radford that recurs in faculty, student, and administrator discussions of the institution is that it is a "party school." Faculty say we must change the party image of Radford, but they are uncertain how to proceed. Students, asked informally whether it in fact *is* a party school, are reported to smile and say, "You don't know the half of it." One student says that the widely understood purpose of the red-beaconed radio tower on the roof of eleven-story Muse Hall is to give drunk students a guide home. "Just look for the Muse," is the advice she gives to what she calls "dazed and confused rookies."

New freshmen, recently quoted by a student newspaper reporter, say that they came to Radford at least partly for its party scene; and one characterizes Radford as a place where "every waking hour, in every room, there was a party going on . . . and no one cared about doing their homework." A recurring bit of folk-myth at Radford is that the university was featured as one of the signal east coast party schools by *Playboy* magazine. In fact, according to the magazine's editorial office, it was not (and Radford was not the only institution from which concerned callers phoned *Playboy* to check), but the insistence of the myth suggests something of the university's uncertain sense of itself.

Whether the image is accurate or not, this much is true: In a 1988 survey of students who withdrew from Radford between 1987 and 1988, the most frequently stated *dis*satisfaction was their perception of it as a party school. Radford faculty frequently say informally that many of their best students transfer to the University of Virginia or James Madison (other state colleges with party reputations of their own but more firmly established academic status). Many of the surveyed students transferred to other colleges and universities with prestigious academic reputations—William and Mary, for example, Loyola, Michigan, UCLA. Recent alumni also report that, though many of them value their Radford degree highly, they believe that others consider it only average. This finding disheartens faculty and administrators here, but it corroborates their own intuitions about the university's public standing.

As an academic institution, Radford does not seem yet to have achieved integrity. Whatever its undeniable success in a number of areas, many of Radford's own faculty regard its academic success as limited. In a recent address to new Radford faculty, the president of the faculty, Tom Mullis, noted his own concern about the academic environment here. Mullis's work as a teacher and his long-standing contributions to the university have earned him one of the annual awards for distinguished Radford faculty, but one element of his message for his new colleagues was caution. He spoke of a lack of patience among students with learning and working to learn. He spoke of his own disappointment and frustration. On the occasion of welcoming teachers new to Radford, he made it a point to recommend that they have realistic expectations about the academic rigor of the school.

Glen Martin, a philosophy professor, has attributed the academic character of Radford to what he considers institutional uncertainty. In a letter to the University Planning Council and in the newsletter of the University Honors Program, Martin has described the state of Radford as "drift." All its parts do not add up, he says. "In spite of many excellent programs and people, the over-all environment at Radford fosters academic mediocrity." According to Martin, the fundamental cause of this institutional drift is that we do not know who we are. A trade school? A technical school? A liberal arts school? There are among us proponents of each definition of ourselves. "But one thing we clearly are *not* (as a whole)," he says, "is an institution focusing on, and committed to, creating a total environment fostering academic and intellectual excellence."

Other internal critics of Radford are more severe. They believe that the overall learning environment is diminished by what one calls the "party mentality" of the school. This same critic goes on to say that even the academic programs which the university strongly supports—among them, Writing Across the Curriculum—"are for many faculty a conscious smokescreen designed to obscure more fundamental institutional failures." In spite of their individual merits, the criticism continues, these programs "may actually be undermining the institution's academic value and integrity."

Such an attitude—of skepticism, cynicism, frustrated purpose, and distrust of the institution's leadership—may help explain the resistance of some faculty to Writing Across the Curriculum. As valuable as the program has been to some, others have regarded it as bogus, just one more component in a public relations campaign. Because the program has been promoted so energetically, it seems to some as misleading as the landscaping. More attention, they say, seems given to the lawns at Radford than to the library, and they ask, angrily and sadly, "Why more money for mulch than for books?" The parallel question: Why a writing-across-the-curriculum program in a university that is not seriously committed to academic work?

One answer is that the program is a *sign* of the institution's commitment. It is not as photogenic as the Dedmon Center or as tangible as the Flossie Martin Art Gallery, but it too has been incorporated into the university's studied image. It has served a valuable symbolic function. It has provided the most striking evidence that Radford's commitment to teaching and learning is in fact serious.

Other images might have been chosen to do this "positioning" work—the Appalachian Studies Program, for example, or, had it been established earlier, the Oral Communication Program. But Writing Across the Curriculum had the scope that other possible candidates lacked. It aimed to influence faculty teaching all courses and thus to extend its benefits to every student at the university. It was also fashionable. In the early eighties, the ideas and name of "writing across the curriculum" were receiving animated coverage in the public press, not just in professional journals. Though its newsworthiness may have passed, however, Radford can claim for its program that it was among the earliest and that it is still one of only a handful of writing-across-the-curriculum programs in Virginia public colleges, and the only one that has been so generously funded by the state.

Perhaps more importantly, the topic itself—writing and the writing ability of students—was and remains the subject of intense public interest. A college that has staked a claim to this topic has a clear public agenda. Everyone knows what it is about. According to some Radford faculty, this is one of the most important benefits Writing Across the Curriculum has rendered to the university: it has given it a clearly communicable academic project.

Colleges need "themes," Dave Albig, the chairperson of Radford's mathematics department, says, "and writing across the curriculum is one of them." The layman can understand and appreciate it. Albig's view is that this kind of theme was particularly important for Radford. As it grew from a teacher-training college to a comprehensive university, the public's image of Radford became less clear. The public needed a more distinct sense of what was going on here, of what the institution was about. According to Albig, Writing Across the Curriculum gave and continues to give it that clear purpose.

Whether this analysis is correct or not, it is fair to say that, since 1982, Radford University has used the Writing Across the Curriculum program more than any other of its features to publicize its academic character. When the university orchestrates its traveling recruitment program every spring to interest new students from around the state, the promotional video it presents highlights Writing Across the Curriculum. At each stop, Donald Dedmon speaks, joking with his audiences as usual and insisting, with characteristic emphasis, on Radford's commitment to teaching and learning. His example? A mathematics teacher (he is referring to Coreen Mett; sometimes he names her, sometimes not) who teaches calculus and who has her students writing all the time—writing to redefine problems, writing to think, writing to learn. A personal example of a particular teacher, but he means her to serve as the image of a program and of an institution.

Critics will not be satisfied that this is anything more than semiotic sleight of hand, signs representing signs. But Mett's classroom is real. So are her homework assignments. So are the papers she has delivered and published describing writing strategies for the teaching of mathematics. So are the years she spent serving as one of the coordinators of Radford's program. If her work is particularly striking because it is unusual—paradoxically using one language to help students learn another, and more actively using writing than many of her colleagues—it is not a less accurate example of committed teaching just because it is good.

When Dedmon points to Mett's work as the work of a creative, resourceful, dedicated teacher and says that hers is the kind Radford University prizes, he is not simply describing what Radford is but sketching what it wants to be. The process of image-making is inseparable from the process of self-definition. Mett's is the kind of teaching to which Radford University aspires. It is the kind Radford encourages; it is the kind it invites students to expect.

"Who are we?" Dedmon asked when he first came to Radford College. "What is our reason for being?" His first answers to these questions were both pragmatic and indefinite. Pragmatic, because the college needed to attract students if it was to survive. Indefinite, because the academic mission had still to evolve. By presenting a vibrant public image—beautiful grounds, a range of appealing extracurricular activities, and a spirited social life—Radford has succeeded in attracting students. Its academic appeal, however, is still being shaped. At present, the Writing Across the Curriculum program—more than any other internal program—is giving that shape public substance. Its work is unambiguously academic. Its focus is the classroom. The question faculty who participate in it repeatedly ask themselves is, "How can we use writing to teach better? How can we use writing to help our students learn better?"

That this program should be publicized so insistently helps define the institution in ways Dedmon forecast when he first came. He wanted to draw students to Radford by whatever means he could. The first year he was here, Radford accepted all but three of the students who applied. But he also wanted to emphasize that the college's primary purpose is the "teaching transaction." The Writing Across the Curriculum program has permitted him, in a way he did not anticipate then, to merge these two desires, to create an image that will attract students to learning.

The public image of Radford as an academic institution may still not be fully distinct, and critics may still say that it is misleading. But everyone will agree that Radford is in the process of developing an academic culture—Dedmon in the public eye, faculty in committees on the "academic environment," teachers and students in myriad, unheralded ways in the classroom. The Writing Across the Curriculum program has thus served the institution doubly. It has helped to foster the university's attention to teaching and learning, and it has so penetrated the university's sense of itself as to make writing one of its central metaphors.

Not surprisingly, this can be seen in a vivid image. For nearly seven years now, the university's public relations literature has carried two graphic motifs: a waving line and a fountain pen. Created by a team of artists in consultation with students, faculty, and administrators at Radford, the image began with an abstract waving line. In order to give the line academic substance, artist David Crowder now explains, he added an emphatic close-up of the tip of a fountain pen. Line and pen were joined in the first version of this image, by photographing the pen writing the word "academic." The waving line thus became the line of written letters, and the tenor of the whole image was of an institution dedicated to academic work.

In the latest version, pen and line appear again, this time under the title, "A Spirit of Change." The glossy cover illustration of the university's most recent prospectus for new students represents a rainbow-colored line rising determinedly into a blue sky. The tip of the fountain pen—again in close-up, sharply detailed, this time vertical—is drawing the central line. Two images thus are merged in one, two themes subliminally equated: the rising trajectory of Radford University is a line of writing.

Chapter Nine

Politics
Power and Persons

The process by which ideas become embodied in institutions is always political. The choice of which ideas will be considered in the first place, then the course they take, the modifications they undergo, and the speed of their development—all these different aspects of the process depend upon the particular political context in which it occurs. In the case of Writing Across the Curriculum at Radford, the political dimensions of the institution and of the program, and the relations among persons and interests within them, have been complex and various. They have not always been clearly recognized.

Some faculty have been insistent about the program's political character. They point out that the way the university has used Writing Across the Curriculum in molding its image is an obvious example. The administration's support of the program, they say, has been unmistakably political, as are the ways the program has been designed and conducted, the reward system with which faculty participation is recognized, even the manner in which the power of the program is understated or underestimated. Other faculty have tended not to think of Writing Across the Curriculum in terms of politics. They find its work valuable to them. They pick up good ideas for their own teaching; they make friends; they write stories or papers that end up getting published. And they are shocked when the political relations of the program are exposed most bluntly.

Both perspectives are part of the program's history, and gradually a composite picture of its political character has emerged.

During a workshop in 1987, Murphy and Self were amazed by a faculty debate about politics which was unprecedented in its intensity and frustration. The dissatisfaction revealed in the debate was perhaps the more marked for them because it came at the end of an otherwise successful and satisfying two weeks of collaborative work. But just so: the success of the program in general had for the most part been achieved without much conscious recognition by them of its political context.

On the last morning, before a catered picnic lunch and a post-workshop softball game, the topic for discussion was the political role of Writing Across the Curriculum in the university. Nursing professor Karma Castleberry conducted the discussion. "What are the implications of this program for the whole university?" she asked. "For faculty who are not here? For departments in which content requirements are strictly set by accreditation agencies or licensing exams? For . . ."

These were the questions she had devised to prompt the group. She did not need to wait long for answers.

"This is a good program," Bill Hrezo said. "I know that *I* have learned a lot from it and that students in my classes have been the beneficiaries. But if class size keeps going up, I know that I won't keep trying the sorts of things I have learned. I taught two writing-intensive courses this year—two sections of Intro to Politics, forty students each—and it near killed me. I don't want to see the university talking out of both sides of its mouth: do more writing in your classes and, by the way, here are ten or fifteen more students for each of your classes."

Others were more emphatic still. One said, "As valuable as this program's promises are, it cannot produce. It claims that we can engage students more deeply in their own learning by using language. But with the numbers of students and the numbers of courses and the committee work and the general indifference to serious intellectual inquiry, those claims are (I hate to have to say it) just a smokescreen."

During the two weeks that had preceded this discussion, a nearly unanimous consensus had developed that the workshop was a success. It provided, some said, an excellent example of how teachers might work with larger classes (there were nearly forty participants in the workshop). Dennis Cogswell, the chairperson of the social work department and an experienced group leader, said that it was a consummate example of successful group management. Clarence Rose, the director of Radford's MBA program, expressed his gratitude for the chance to use the workshop to write an article on new changes in the federal tax law. Everything seemed to work, discussions, writing, writing groups, social interaction among faculty new to one another.

But the dissatisfaction voiced in Karma Castleberry's session was unmistakable. Some participants were impatient with success; they wanted to use the program's momentum to challenge the university administration to institute radical academic reform. "This is an influential group," one speaker said. "Here in this room are some of the most widely respected teachers on campus. This program has power. Why don't we use it? Why allow ourselves to be co-opted by the administration?" It was never clear what specific changes (other than reducing class size) the most vocal speakers had in mind, and it never became clear just how co-opted the group in general thought they were. But the dissatisfaction was deep and vehemently expressed. The political stance of the program was much too modest for them, its apparently a-political attitude foolishly naive.

Looking back on that moment now, Self and Murphy admit that they were less politically candid than some of those speakers. In five years, they had never talked about the program between themselves—and now think they did not wish to understand it—in terms of power. As for method, they never thought that confrontation—either with the faculty or the administration—would yield useful results of the kind the program was designed to foster. Further, they believed that to use the program as some of the speakers were suggesting, as a sort of political action committee, would weaken its own work. They were repelled by the straightforward suggestion that, once having accrued influence by cooperation, they should use it combatively. Though in fact Murphy and Self said little during the discussion, one frustrated speaker later expressed his disgust: "Rich and Warren just took the program back from us." The workshop ended with the scheduled party and softball game, and the moderate course of the program continued as before.

Some of the faculty who spoke most forcefully that morning about power have since withdrawn entirely from the program and view it as politically bankrupt. As for Self and Murphy, the directness and passion of that last discussion surprised and disoriented them. They had not realized that so close to the surface of the program were volatile frustration and anger. If their conduct of it thereafter did not change markedly, however, they now believe their attitude did. For the first time that either of them can remember, they were forced to confront the political reality—even in their own actions and decisions—that they had earlier largely ignored.

From the start, whether Murphy and Self recognized or acknowledged it, the program design itself had a political character. It had no director, no office, no center separate from the persons involved in it. Once the resource library was established, for example, it kept moving from place to place. For a while, it was in the Writing Center, then in Murphy's office, then in Kirby's, then in the office of the secretary assigned part-time to the program. The inconvenience this wandering created for anyone who wanted to borrow a book or just browse was offset, in the minds of coordinators, by its symbolic value: Writing Across the Curriculum does not belong in any one place; it is everywhere. Even as it expanded and more people were recruited to serve as coordinators of different parts of the program— facilitating faculty travel, organizing the weekend workshops, editing the newsletter—the leadership remained cooperative. Only recently, and only reluctantly, has any effort been made to identify one person who is ultimately responsible for directing the whole.

This relatively egalitarian, informal organization, however, has been to some extent illusory. It has both invited equal participation and sometimes concentrated exclusive authority in particular individuals. Susan Kirby, for example, was not included in the first team of coordinators. She had helped conduct the earliest faculty colloquies, even before the program officially began, and she was its newsletter editor from the start. But Murphy and Self worked together without involving her in planning or proposal writing or negotiating with the administration. They arrogated to themselves the roles of co-coordinators of the program, and they were soon regarded—by faculty and administration, by Kirby herself—as the directors of the program.

For five years, the two shared equal responsibility for its direction. But even when a faculty advisory council was formed or new faculty accepted coordinator roles, one or the other of the co-founders was still regarded as the undesignated head coordinator. When Murphy resigned his position, first to go on academic leave, then to return to full-time teaching, Self became the generally acknowledged, though still unofficial, director of the program. In the spring of 1990, the importance of his role became particularly clear. His other duties as chair of the English department had become so pressing that he announced his need to resign from his coordinating responsibilities. No one of the other faculty involved in running the program felt able at the time to assume the job of being head coordinator. Had Self not then agreed to continue indefinitely, it is not clear how such structure as the program had would have been maintained.

The importance of his leadership is evident, too, in what has happened since. As the director of the Office of Academic Enrichment Programs, he is no longer a coordinator of the Writing Across the Curriculum program. Yet he continues to influence its work. He meets with coordinators to discuss their plans. He serves as unofficial liaison between the program and the vice-president's and president's offices. The administration still regards him as central to the program. And the faculty who now coordinate it still look to him—not surprisingly, after many years of leadership—for personal, if not official approval, in designing activities and budgeting funds.

In spite of the desire of some faculty, therefore—even of Murphy and Self—to imagine the program as a-political, it has continually operated within a tacit hierarchy of authority and influence. Further, its earliest planning deliberately took into account the political relations among academic departments and between the faculty and administration. A calculated effort was made to involve faculty from as many other departments besides English as possible. This caused resentment among some members of the English department who considered themselves neglected. But even when such unintended reactions became clear to Self and Murphy, they continued to emphasize the participation of faculty outside their department in order to reinforce the cross-curricular character of the program. When they were planning panel discussion schedules or weekend workshop groups or writing-intensive course offerings, they compiled lists of the department and college affiliations of participating faculty, and deliberately sought to foster faculty involvement that would be "representative."

They were very careful, too, about the aegis of the program. Because the first funding they sought from the University Foundation was a "faculty-development" grant, they characterized the program from the start as a "faculty-development" project. They could not have anticipated how useful such a designation would later be. When the program emphasis gradually broadened from writing to teaching and learning, the original label continued to serve. When debate arose over the nature and purpose of writing-intensive courses, it was resolved in light of the program's continuing focus on faculty development. Writing-intensive courses were thus conceived, not as curricular requirements, but as opportunities for faculty to experiment with uses of writing that might enhance their teaching in all their courses. When informal program evaluations were undertaken, the "faculty-development" nature of the program shifted the evaluation focus. Instead of attempting to assess changes in student writing (which no writing-across-the-curriculum program has yet been able to measure successfully), the program was able to focus on changes in faculty teaching.

The faculty emphasis of the program was something both Self and Murphy were careful to stress from the beginning. They knew—part common sense, part experience with Writing Project inservice programs in which school administrators forced teachers to "participate"—that they wanted the program to be voluntary and to be faculty-initiated. They asked the university president not to mandate the program they had proposed. They wrote to him that, though his support was essential, the program would need to be guided by faculty concerns and driven by faculty energy. If it were to inspire the imaginative involvement and commitment of people, they argued that it could not be imposed. He agreed, and from the beginning he has made a concerted public effort to disassociate himself from its management or leadership. He called generally for more writing in 1982, but it was a faculty-designed and -conducted program that resulted. When Self and Murphy proposed the idea of writing-intensive courses in 1986, they suggested that Dedmon merely indicate the possible value of such courses. Again he agreed and, except for a brief mention in his next convocation speech, left the faculty to work out whether, what, how, and why such courses might be implemented. In general, Murphy and Self were anxious that the program be conducted under the aegis of the faculty. They asked the president to permit it to grow and develop, visibly, on its own, and he has from the start done just that.

Yet the president has supported the program in many ways that have strengthened its political presence in the institution. He and his executive assistant and the vice-president for Academic Affairs, for example, have always regarded program requests as meritorious and have readily granted them. Before there was any money in the program budget for faculty travel, David Moore agreed to send four faculty to a seminar on writing across the curriculum at the University of Chicago. When, during a faculty writing workshop on campus, the coordinators realized that they wanted to be able to print up everyone's writing in a group collection and have it ready to distribute the next morning, Charles Wood asked the university printing office to keep someone available on overtime to do the job. On the way to one weekend workshop, a university van broke down; a call to the president's office immediately brought out a maintenance crew with a new van so the faculty could go on to their work. Except where the program has needed to follow the strict accounting procedures required of all state institutions, it has been freed of red tape. Whenever it has needed administrative help, that help has been given without hesitation or reserve.

Susan Kirby tells a story of such help that suggests the political status of Writing Across the Curriculum at Radford. When she brought the first pasted-up copy of the newsletter, *Writing & Learning*, to the university printing office in 1982, she was told that it could not be photocopied without the permission of the Public Information Office. Any publication to be distributed under the university's name, she was told, had to be approved by Deborah Brown, the director of public information. When Kirby sought permission, however, Brown immediately granted it, without even reading the copy. She told Kirby, too, that subsequent issues could be printed without her prior approval. "I see that gesture," Kirby now says, "as symbolic of the administration's carte blanche approval of Writing Across the Curriculum." On the one hand, the university's standing policy was designed to ensure that the right image of itself would be projected in all communications. On the other, it had enough confidence in the program to grant it a blanket exception.

The university also reinforced the program's independence by allowing it to develop freely. Even when plans have been made that have not been implemented, the university has respected the program's autonomy. With the help of other faculty, for example, Murphy and Self decided—after having proposed otherwise—that writing-intensive courses ought *not* to be required; the administration simply accepted this change. A proposed state-wide conference for the presentation of student academic writing and symposia on writing and learning was never carried out. Its omission was not questioned. The administration has regarded the decisions of faculty participating in the program as completely reliable. This regard has not only given them confidence in their ability and in the value of their work as teachers but also reinforced the program's political status in the institution.

The success of Radford's Writing Across the Curriculum program, in other words, has depended in part on a complex web of political relations. These relations have been built up quietly, over time. Often they extend beyond the university community. Sometimes they are so intertwined with other elements as to be—at least to some—almost inconspicuous. In 1985, for example, Dedmon asked the two coordinators to meet with the Board of Visitors to explain the program. He gave them no guidelines, just an invitation, and free rein to say or do whatever they thought best. When a newly appointed State Secretary of Education visited Radford in 1987, the president invited the coordinators to his office to talk informally with the Secretary about the program.

Murphy and Self interpreted these invitations as expressing the president's confidence both in the program and in their ability to characterize its spirit and importance. More than that: he seemed to them to be asking for help. So they approached these meetings personally as, in general, they approached the program. They were glad to have been asked. They talked animatedly about what they thought. They both now think they must have recognized the political bearing of what was happening, but that seemed secondary to them. Of more concern in their minds was the opportunity to represent with clarity and enthusiasm what they and their colleagues were up to.

The political relations within which the program developed were often personal and social as well. In February of 1988, Nancy Martin conducted a late-afternoon discussion for faculty and area school teachers at what was called, in her honor, "tea."

Perhaps two dozen teachers gathered themselves into a loose circle in a high-ceilinged, large-windowed room on the second floor of Walker Hall. From her oblique perch on the edge of a straight chair, Martin reviewed some of the theoretical issues she considered pressing for teachers. She spoke from brief notes, then stopped again and again to say, "Would anybody like to come in on that? I should like for someone to comment on that." They did.

Philosophy professor Glen Martin spoke about his repeated frustration trying to urge his students to write about what they were learning, to take it seriously, to consider it important. Nancy Martin listened, said, "Yes," acknowledging as she always does the difficulties of individual teachers in particular teaching situations. Then she asked, with equal candor, "*Is* it important? What they're doing? What you're asking them to do? *Are* they learning something valuable?" Everyone in the room felt her questions penetrate.

Among the participants in that afternoon discussion was Joyce Graham, a public high school teacher from the small neighboring community of Shawsville, Virginia. Herself a Radford College graduate, Graham took her undergraduate degree in 1976 with an emphasis in secondary English teaching, following the same course as generations of earlier Radford women into education. Graham's political relationship with Radford, however, has been unique. First she graduated as president of the student government; later she was appointed to the Radford University Board of Visitors.

On the afternoon of the tea for Nancy Martin, Graham had been invited, along with the other members of the Board, to dinner at the president's home. She arrived late. "I came to the workshop expecting to stay a half hour," she later explained. "But I think I was one of the last people to leave. I was fascinated with Nancy Martin, spellbound by her, and by the feeling that had been created in that room."

Remembering that evening and appreciating its serendipitous political character, Graham still laughs. It was already after 6:00 when she walked in the front door of the president's house and into the company of the other members of the Board and all the vice-presidents and their spouses. Graham apologized to Dedmon, told him about the workshop, wanted him to know what she had just seen and heard.

Then the president stopped her, tapped his glass with an hors d'oeuvres knife, and asked her to explain to them all what she had just been telling him.

"I felt very exhilarated about the kinds of things I had heard," she says now, remembering. "I tried to describe how exciting it had been for me to see people really taking the time to look seriously at their own teaching and at their own connections with their students."

What she had meant to be a private explanation was suddenly public, directed not to the president but to her colleagues on the governing board of the university: the truth was that the faculty discussion was so completely absorbing to her, she did not want to pull herself away.

Sometimes the political fortunes of Writing Across the Curriculum have depended on moments like this one, invisible to most members of the university community. Sometimes, they depend on the way the president decides—in any given moment—to represent the program and the university to the state.

A story is told, for example, of his appearance one year before the State Senate Finance Committee to speak on behalf of Radford's budget requests for the next two-year period. The hearing Dedmon was attending was designed for state college and university presidents to advocate programs at their institutions that they especially wanted to see supported in the budget. Writing Across the Curriculum was a high priority on Dedmon's advocacy list, and he waited the better part of a day to make his arguments on its behalf.

All the presidents were scheduled to speak. Each had five minutes to present whatever he or she wanted to say. While one president spoke at the lectern, others whispered to their staffs, made notes, prepared their own remarks, came in and out of the room. Up at their desks, the committee listened, read documents, sent and received messages from staff members. Many of the presidents who took the floor did not remain within their five-minute limit. General comments about the importance of higher education, the pressures of enrollment trends, and the dangers of short-sighted budget cutbacks were made so often that the speakers became indistinguishable. Dedmon revised his prepared remarks; then he revised them again. By the time it was his turn, the room was weary with speeches. He took one more look at his notes, rose to approach the lectern, and changed his mind yet again.

This was the one formal presentation he would be permitted all year of Radford University's budget needs for the biennium and of the importance of its Writing Across the Curriculum program. He decided to disregard his speech altogether. He used only a fraction of his allotted five minutes.

"We hoped to be scheduled earlier in the day . . ." he said, according to the story. Though Radford had sent its request for time to Richmond as early as possible, he was far down on the final hearing agenda. He attributed this fact to Radford's geographical location in the far southwest of the state, traditionally its least politically influential region. And he turned this understood disadvantage into a joke.

"We hoped to be scheduled earlier in the day," he said, "but the stagecoach through Radford is running even less reliably than usual."

The room shook itself awake with a burst of laughter.

Then he said that he would not take up the committee members' time with any more requests. He simply wanted to thank them for their support over the years of Radford's many attempts to achieve excellence through innovative programs. Their help was essential and, he assured them, very much appreciated. Then, without mentioning Writing Across the Curriculum at all, he sat down. When the budget allocations were announced, the program had been funded fully for yet another biennium.

Such a story does not surprise those faculty who have always assumed that Writing Across the Curriculum is in the political interests of the university. Nor does it surprise those who understand—however a-political they may imagine it to be at home—that the program has for years been functioning in the competitive political arena of the state legislature. Still, there are those who have supposed that they are involved in a program without political ramifications.

At least two explanations may be offered for this attitude which, however ingenuous, has had an important influence on the development of Writing Across the Curriculum at Radford. The first is that some program participants seem to have equated politics with structure. Minimizing the one, they assumed, automatically minimized the other.

In 1986, confronted with the question of whether the Writing Across the Curriculum program should expand or reduce its structure, anthropologist Melinda Wagner argued that it *needs* a structure. She was speaking from experience. As a practicing field researcher and professional writer, she meant that *she* needs it. It gives her a point of reference, an opportunity, she gets nowhere else. It gives her what her professional discipline seems to deny her: permission to be a teacher. It brings her together with colleagues and friends to talk about what—she confessed—she would not otherwise talk about, even though she considers it essential: teaching and learning in her classroom. Some structured events, some apparatus—panel discussions, workshops, the newsletter, whatever—*something* is necessary, she said: "To *re-mind*."

Wagner's argument is the personal version of the blunter political claim, made informally by the University of Michigan's Jay Robinson: "If you don't have a line-item in the budget, you got nothing." He was talking with Murphy about the political status of writing-across-the-curriculum programs. So long as the concern with writing is fashionable, Robinson argued, or so long as the administrators who originally supported the program are still in office, its continuation may remain reasonably secure. But without institutional security, any program runs the very high risk of being washed out. Robinson, too, was speaking from experience. In the budget crises faced by Michigan in the early 1980s, only the firm institutional establishment of the English Composition Board (the site of Michigan's cross-curricular writing program) saved it from disastrous funding cuts.

But even when the institutional security of Writing Across the Curriculum at Radford seemed for a moment in jeopardy, its faculty coordinators and the members of its advisory council were ambivalent about structure. In 1987, a proposal circulated at Radford sketching what was called a Center for Communication Studies. The projected proposal stressed the application of "new research knowledge" to teaching, and it suggested that the Writing Across the Curriculum program's resources and activities might fall under its umbrella.

When faculty actively involved in Writing Across the Curriculum saw the sketch, they were alarmed. They met and quickly concluded that such a Center for Communication Studies would expropriate the work of Writing Across the Curriculum and redirect its emphases away from faculty dialogue and toward research. They decided to propose a center of their own. As they drafted it, this alternative center amounted to little more than a change of name for Writing Across the Curriculum. It would be, as it had been, "administered independently of all departments and colleges" and "coordinated by a small interdisciplinary team of faculty." In other words, it would maintain precisely the ad hoc structure it had always had. But with one major difference: called the "Center for Writing and Learning," it would for the first time appear on the organizational chart of the university. With a "structure" of its own, the advisory council thought, it would be protected from absorption by other departments or programs in the university bureaucracy.

As it turned out, both their alarm and their work in drafting a new proposal were probably unnecessary. The "Center for Communication Studies" was never approved or established. The "Center for Writing and Learning," on the other hand, *was* approved, but it was never implemented. Once the apparent political need for it was past, the faculty involved in proposing it did nothing to put it into effect. Again, it seemed to them, the less structure the better. And in this particular case, since the "Center" was a purely political construct in the first place, the less structure the less politics.

A second reason for the a-political attitude of some faculty is their desire to understate or underestimate the political power of the program. Power has seemed antithetical to its purposes. Given the fact that its central work has seemed to be the voluntary interaction of teachers with one another and with students in thinking about writing and learning, power has seemed somehow beside the point. At the 1987 conference of the National Council of Teachers of English, Murphy delivered a paper in a session organized to consider the institutionalization of writing across the curriculum. In it, he argued that programs ought to strive to create communities of persons. He based this argument largely on the quixotic conviction that politics is incompatible with mind and heart. But he was looking forward, arguing aloud with himself about how Radford's program ought to evolve, instead of looking back and seeing how important a role power had played in the program all along, even in the experience of individual faculty.

Some time later, a colleague phoned Murphy to ask for a letter commending her involvement in Writing Across the Curriculum. She was applying for promotion, she said, and thought such a letter would help strengthen her dossier. The call brought home to Murphy in a new way the entanglement of power and self-interest and the program's purposes.

The impression is widespread among faculty that participation in Writing Across the Curriculum is strongly supported by the university administration. Faculty involved in the program seem to get special attention when merit evaluations are conducted. The university's annual teaching prizes also seem to provide evidence of the program's special favor. Of the current coordinators, three have been selected for faculty awards, and during the life of the program, half of all the prizes have gone to faculty who have been actively involved in Writing Across the Curriculum. This fact in itself has confirmed for some the university's intention to support the program and its work with tangible rewards. Thus—one small example—the phone call asking for a letter of reference.

"Remind me of what you've done, will you?" Murphy asked.

"Well, I went to two workshops," the caller replied, "and I went to a conference . . ."

Trying to remember, Murphy asked for more detail: "Who led the workshops you attended?"

"I don't remember," she said.

"OK. Well, when were they held?"

"Oh, the first, I don't know. But I think you were there."

"And the conference trip . . . ? Who arranged that with you?" Maybe some other program coordinator had worked more closely with the caller and might be able to write a more persuasive letter.

"I don't know."

"When you came back from the conference, did you write something about it for the newsletter?"

"No," the caller said. "I was going to, but they didn't need any articles then."

"OK . . . Well, I don't remember very clearly these activities you mention. Maybe you worked more closely with someone else. . . ."

The caller tried to help. "You asked me if I wanted to teach a writing-intensive course. Do you remember?"

"Yes." He remembered.

"Well," said the caller, "I couldn't do it then and had to say 'no.' Do you remember?"

"Yes."

Faculty closely involved with Writing Across the Curriculum at Radford still argue with one another about its political character. In interviews and group discussions, they voice very different perceptions of it and attitudes toward it. Sometimes, their voices sound as intense and frustrated as those of the faculty at the workshop in 1987. In spite of all the benefit they have received from the program, some will not deny the cynicism they feel about its political uncertainty. Others cannot reconcile their own joy and satisfaction with what sounds like bitterness in their colleagues.

For all the political dimensions of its growth, one argument goes, the Writing Across the Curriculum program has actually no political power at all. It could be dissolved at virtually any time. As easily as the message went out from the president's office in 1982 that this was a high priority item, a new message could be issued that Writing Across the Curriculum has served its purpose. More likely, the messages could stop altogether: no mention in the convocation or Quest speeches, no reference in recruitment publicity, no credit for faculty participation, no easy access to facilities or funds. For these and many other signs of the program's political strength at Radford have come from the president himself. His sense of the program's value, some say, has given it staying power; at his pleasure it has done its work. This is not politics, one faculty member says, but paternalism. According to this view, Writing Across the Curriculum at Radford is not something to be reckoned with, just something to be used. When its usefulness ends, the argument goes, so will the program.

Faculty who are more hopeful agree, but for different reasons. Though they believe that if the Writing Across the Curriculum program stops being useful it *should* end, they take a broader and more positive view of "useful." They see clearly the public relations benefit of the program, but they also see its benefit to faculty and students, to the academic community, and to the culture of the university. They recognize that the political independence of the program is limited, that its very existence as a "program" depends upon administrative support. But they also believe that political power extends beyond funding or official recognition in university public relations materials.

From the way Radford's Writing Across the Curriculum program was first designed and proposed to the way it is now coordinated and conducted; from the ways it has been encouraged, highlighted, praised, and advocated to the ways it has been bureaucratically protected; from the ways it has welcomed divergent points of view about teaching and learning even to the ways it has entertained different attitudes toward its own politics—nearly everything about it now seems clearly enmeshed in a political fabric.

Even writing about it is a political act. Description inevitably involves selection. What is said and what is not said, which features and events are highlighted and which are de-emphasized, which individuals are named and which go unnamed—all of these decisions have implications; all affect the texture and impact of the account. Certainly any detailed description of an academic program and the institution within which it operates involves such selection and is not without political effects. It may come to function as what Sara Lawrence Lightfoot calls "an organizational text," at once portraying and shaping the perspectives and values of individual members and contributing to the organization's self-definition. It may serve as a catalyst for changes in practice and policy within and beyond the particular institution.

The politics of description, however, need not imply conscious intention. In the early years of the program, for example, Murphy and Self prepared annual reports, first for the University Foundation, then for the president. In these reports, they detailed all the program activities during the year, including appendices with a final budget, copies of all the newsletters, and copies of whatever other in-house Writing Across the Curriculum publications had been produced. They were meant to inform: "Two presentations were made by outside consultants and six panel discussions were conducted by Radford University faculty and students. . . . Nineteen faculty members from departments across the university participated in a weekend workshop. . . . Several faculty were invited this year to serve as consultants at other schools and colleges interested in developing writing-across-the-curriculum programs" (1986).

When Murphy and Self first began to write these reports they did not make fully explicit to themselves their other purposes. In addition to reporting, they were trying to persuade, to instruct, to influence the president's understanding of, and commitment to, the program. When, in 1985, for example, they wrote about his support of the program, they linked it with, and subordinated it to, the faculty's thought and experience:

> Such strength as [the program] has derives from its two most important features.
>
> First . . . no other writing-across-the-curriculum program we know of receives such strong institutional funding and such unambiguous support from the highest levels of the administration. Writing, reading, studying, learning—Radford faculty are being encouraged to do all of these . . . in order to strengthen their teaching and thereby enrich the intellectual experience of Radford's students.
>
> Second, it is a faculty-based program, developed and conducted by them, guided by their commitment to their own discipline and animated by their dedication to teaching. The program is not being imported from outside; it is not following a formulaic agenda; it is not limited to a group of certain faculty or certain academic fields. In every way we can think of we are inviting the participation of every faculty member at Radford, and the shape of the program is emerging in response to their participation. *They* are writing across the curriculum; there is no other.

Murphy and Self called this a "report," but it was more than that. It was a rhetorical statement, a fiction, a story they were telling themselves and the university's president. The story went beyond his office, they now know. It went to the Board of Visitors directly, and indirectly, in Dedmon's speeches, to the state legislature, to the faculty, to parents and students. Even if the writers did not fully recognize or acknowledge what they were doing, therefore, their writing was political. They were trying to fix—not in the bureaucratic structure of the institution but in their own minds and in the mind of the president—an idea of what both the program and the university might be.

Chapter Ten

Academic Culture and the Spirit of Change

Professor Chuck Kugler's office at Radford University is crowded, narrow, and bright. Originally a washroom, it is little larger than a supply closet and now serves as Kugler's combination study and laboratory: counter, sink (one relic of its earlier life), tall wooden book cases filled with biology textbooks and stacks of issues of *Evolution*, *Systematic Zoology*, *Journal of College Science Teaching*, and *Psyche*, an 1874 leather-bound second edition of Darwin's *Descent of Man*, two desks. Kugler laughs and explains: "That's research; this is teaching." He moves back and forth the short distance between them on a stenographer's chair—to the one where he prepares lectures for his general biology and evolution classes, then to the other under the high wooden window, on which he keeps his phase-contrast and dissection Zeiss microscopes and the ant specimens he is immediately working on.

It is the week after graduation. Kugler is seated in front of a Macintosh on a moveable computer stand in the middle of the room. He is writing notes to himself about the upper division course in evolution he has just finished teaching. Speculating; wondering; thinking aloud about alternate readings ("Replace Williams article— with Radner and Radner section?") and alternate assignments ("Instead of second paper have students write letters to each other asking questions and explaining.").

The details of Kugler's notes and of the cramped space in which he is writing them provide a useful counterpoint to the professional literature on writing across the curriculum in American colleges and universities.

Kugler is an entomologist, specializing in the comparative anatomy of ants. A visitor struck by the bright light of his office soon sees that he needs it for his work. His research requires not only that he examine exceedingly tiny anatomical parts of already small mechanisms but also that he draw painstakingly exact illustrations of them to accompany his written reports. Each of the hundreds of drawings he inks must first be penciled, then traced on translucent mylar, then touched up with a still finer rapidograph pen so that the lines are as smooth as possible. Sometimes this precise finish requires the additional step of painting an exact edge on the inked lines with white paint. Occasionally, he must then shave away a sliver of the white paint with a scalpel. Such drawings are a necessary part of Kugler's work. Readers need them to understand the comparisons he is making among species. But Kugler points out that the real reason the drawings are important is that they make him *see*. In order to draw an ant sting, he says, "I have to see it absolutely exactly."

Taxonomic drawing requires much more precision than the portrait of a writing-across-the-curriculum program or the academic culture in which it works. But it is certainly true that in order to draw either, one needs to *see*. The professional literature on writing across the curriculum has tended to make seeing difficult. In attempting to generalize, it has tended to schematize programs, reducing them to statements of ideas or lists of features that easily become clichéd in their abstraction. Even where the texture of particular programs has been represented more fully, their description is most often abbreviated and their vitality diminished. Thus, the story of their implementation has almost never been told, and the complex interaction between idea and institution has remained largely unexplored.

Many good reasons can account for this situation—among them, limited publication space, the desire to provide a broad overview of the writing-across-the-curriculum movement, and the fact that the programs at many schools *do* have similar features. Still, schematic descriptions mislead and may have contributed to some of the serious failures institutions have encountered when they have tried to establish programs of their own.

In a 1985 report of a survey of writing-across-the-curriculum programs, C. W. Griffin discussed the "limited number of elements that make them up—writing centers, faculty workshops, and courses of various kinds. Some programs are based on one of these elements," Griffin says; "others combine them in some fashion" ("Programs for Writing Across the Curriculum: A Report," *College Composition and Communication* 36 [1985]: 400). Susan McLeod has conducted a follow-up survey to Griffin's and has analyzed the results in order to "paint a larger picture of the WAC movement in the late 1980s" ("Writing Across the Curriculum: The Second Stage and Beyond," *College Composition and Communication 40 [1989]: 337).* Her report discusses types of funding, varieties of faculty workshops, what she calls the "crop of WAC newsletters" (340), writing-intensive courses, and the different administrative structures within which some writing-across-the-curriculum programs have been embodied. But because theirs are summary reports, neither Griffin nor McLeod is able to give much more than a sentence (more often a phrase) to the features of any one program.

The brevity of their descriptions tend to make even very different programs appear similar. The more abstractly the features of a writing-across-the-curriculum program are delineated, the more common they seem. Griffin concludes his survey summary, for example, with the acknowledgment that writing-across-the-curriculum programs differ widely. Then he claims that "most have something in common—the premises on which they are based": that writing skills must be practiced and reinforced throughout the curriculum; that to write is to learn; and that the responsibility for the quality of student writing is university-wide (402-3). Susan McLeod warns against homogenization, the blandness of "taking a vital new idea and making it into something more like familiar structures and programs" (342). But then her own account itemizes the familiar: workshops, released time, newsletters, internal funding, free lunches, and "the now-familiar 'writing-intensive' courses" (341). The danger of such lists—of premises or features—is that they seem to add up to writing across the curriculum. They seem—because it is so difficult to define the idea in practice otherwise—to *be* writing across the curriculum. Like the paintings of Rene Magritte, but without his ironic distance, they seem to say, "This *is* a pipe."

A more extended treatment of writing-across-the-curriculum programs—and one that underlines their heterogeneity—is offered by Toby Fulwiler and Art Young in *Programs That Work: Models and Methods for Writing Across the Curriculum* (Portsmouth, NH: Boynton/Cook, 1990). In it, they collect the self-descriptions of fourteen writing-across-the-curriculum programs the editors regard as successful. The effect on readers is immediate: "success" is relative; "programs" are context-specific; writing across the curriculum "works" in a multitude of ways. Still, Fulwiler and Young themselves generalize—about the "remarkably similar goals" and the "common core" of language theory most programs share; about the most frequent administrative questions and the most common institutional "enemies" of writing across the curriculum. On the one hand, therefore, they say and show that programs are different, and on the other they suggest that the experiences of establishing and conducting them, are, in important and useful ways, similar.

Institutionalizing an idea, however, is always a complex, always an idiosyncratic, process. The "idea" itself is transformed as it is interpreted and used by individuals. The needs and purposes of those individuals, as well as their imagination and energy, shape their understanding of the idea and of the ways it may be implemented. The history and character of the particular institution, its culture, its sense of itself and of its mission—all of these constrain or enable the institutional forms in which the idea may be embodied. Any college or university that wishes to establish a writing-across-the-curriculum program, therefore, would do well to take Richard Young's recent advice: "Programs should be shaped to fit the institutional environment." It is "risky to use one program as a model for another. The better adapted a program is to its environment, the less appropriate it is to copy it in other environments" ("Designing for Change in a Writing-Across-The-Curriculum Program," *Balancing Acts,* ed. Virginia Chappell, Mary Louise-Meissner, Chris Anderson [Carbondale, IL: Southern Illinois UP, 1991] 146).

It is certainly the misappropriation of models that Edward White blames for the spectacular failure of writing-across-the-curriculum programs at four American colleges and universities. In "The Damage of Innovations Set Adrift," White describes the establishment of "writing-intensive courses" at a large eastern state university (*American Association for Higher Education Bulletin* 43.3 [1990]: 3–5). Three such courses would be required of each student for the baccalaureate degree. To support the program, the administration announced a new faculty development project, promised funding for an improved writing center, placed enrollment caps of twenty on the writing-intensive courses, and proposed an ongoing assessment procedure.

Five years later, when White was brought in as a consultant-evaluator to assess the program, he found it a shambles. Two of the essential support structures for the program—the faculty development project and the writing center—had been sacrificed in a budget cut. A new administration had lost interest in the ongoing assessment process. The twenty student enrollment cap had been ignored by department chairs whose budgets depended on head counts in their courses. So few writing-intensive courses were actually being offered that, with the three-course degree requirement in place, the average enrollments had risen to over fifty. And with these numbers—and no faculty development program to assist teachers in exploring ways to use writing in the classroom—very little writing was actually going on in these courses. Indeed, students from the writing-intensive courses interviewed by the evaluator confessed that they had no idea what the "WI" designation stood for. Meanwhile, faculty teaching the traditional courses had sharply decreased the amount of writing in their classes, believing that their designated colleagues were now responsible for this task. "The net result of the new writing program," White concludes, was "less writing throughout the curriculum, cynical faculty, mocking students, graduates even less prepared to do critical thinking and writing than before" (3).

This is only one of four stories White tells. All discourage. All illustrate ambitious and laudable purposes gone sadly awry. Stories of failure are no more homogeneous than stories of success, but White draws from these four different failures at least one common theme. In each case, the institution tried to implement a successful program without fully understanding either it or itself. In each, White says, the problems that resulted were caused "by importing even excellent ideas from other institutions without understanding the substructures that allow the ideas to flourish" (5). All four stories illustrate what White calls "a sure formula for failure: Imagine that ideas that work elsewhere will solve your problems quickly and inexpensively, without building support and substructures, without prolonged attention. Without substructures, built with care on campus, the new idea will fail" (5).

Elaine Maimon—the founder of Beaver College's writing-across-the-curriculum program, one of the very first such programs in American colleges—voices a concern similar to White's. No institution, she writes in the Beaver College chapter of *Programs That Work*, should "import procedures without examining their consequences in another setting." Descriptions of writing across the curriculum "can suggest only general principles, not formulas, prescriptions, or tricks." Such care is necessary because "each college, university, or school has its own identity and history that must be taken into account when planning for change of any sort." Rather than assuming that writing across the curriculum is homogeneous or its ideas and features portable, "curriculum planners should function as ethnographers, studying the traditions and mores of their own distinct communities" (Portsmouth, NH: Boynton/Cook, 1990, 138).

The description we have undertaken here of Radford University does not claim to be ethnography, strictly speaking, but it has sought to identify some of the central traditions and mores of its academic culture and to represent at least some of its minds at work.

For example, Chuck Kugler, thinking aloud at his Macintosh the week after graduation: "First paper and handouts to focus attention were great. Students seemed much more prepared for discussion than last year when they were given verbal instructions and only took notes." On the walls of Kugler's office are decorations that reflect his preoccupations: a Nature Company photographic print of wild, fragile eggs (one of which has been painted to suggest the earth); a Sierra Club print of Alpine wildflowers; on the wall corner just inside his door, a 700-million-year graph of life, the "Tower of Time," painted by John Gurche for the National Museum of Natural History; and taped over his "teaching" desk, a photocopied sheet of suggested writing activities:

SOME WRITING-TO-LEARN STRATEGIES

WRITING TO:	SUGGESTED TEACHER INSTRUCTIONS
1. Discover what one does or doesn't already know	Write down what you already know about the process of photosynthesis.
2. Assemble information by taking notes and making notes about subject matter	Draw a line down the center of your paper. On the left side, take notes on the important concepts you read in Chapter 12. On the right side, make a personal note about each recorded note. (React to, rephrase, respond to, question, or associate the ideas with something you know.)
3. Predict what will happen next in the text	Now that you have read about lungs, what do you need to know next? What do you think will come next in the chapter?
4. Paraphrase, translate, or rephrase the text	There are ten sections in Chapter 12. After receiving a number from one to ten, rephrase your respective section in your own words. Tomorrow we will read our own versions of Chapter 12.
5. Associate images, events, ideas, or personal experiences with subject matter	When you think about the Declaration of Independence, what do you see (images, events, ideas, or even a personal experience that reminds you of that time in our history)?
6. Define concepts or ideas about subject matter	In your own words, define the terms in bold print found in the second section of Chapter 12.
7. React or respond to texts or discussions	Take the last five minutes of class to write down the most important ideas for you in our discussion.
8. Create problems to be solved with subject matter	Make up a word problem that reflects a real-life situation in which the solver would have to use the formula for finding the area of a rectangle.

(Judy Self, *Plain Talk*, Virginia Department of Education, 1987, 16)

"I keep that up there to remind myself of things I can try," he tells a visitor.

He means in his teaching, but he might just as well be describing the notes he is writing to himself today about the evolution course he has just completed:

> Second paper did force students to reconsider the articles, rather than just drop them as in previous year, but had problems:
> a) Students fell into the habit of basically using their first paper and sprinkling in a few comments about the discussion. I'm not sure they really returned to the text and reevaluated it.
> b) Took a lot of extra time on my part and I presume on theirs for dubious benefit.
> c) Students complained that there were too many papers [ten], especially since they had to be typed and were only worth 5 points. Several suggested they should be extra credit.

The notes continue. What happened? Why? How well did it work? Kugler writes to himself also about the informal evaluation of a colleague who audited the course. What could be done differently?

> Paper Ideas—
> could allow *first paper* to be handwritten—either answers to questions or comparison sheets of Ho [hypothesis], Evid [evidence] and argument, and Assumpt[ions]. This would perhaps lessen the stress, make it feel like they were writing less papers, and send the message that this is not a final product, and thus it can be (should be) changed on the second paper. . . .
> The risk is that the students will be less prepared for the discussion, because they have only taken notes, not tried to put their ideas together. For that reason I should try to make the first draft not just note-taking, but question-answering as I did this year. . . .

We can hear Kugler's mind surge in the elliptical structure of these sentences. We can mark his uncertainty in the qualifiers ("perhaps") and modal auxiliaries ("would," "could"). His notes trace some of his own emotional experience ("a lot of extra time") and try to calculate the psychological experience of students ("This would perhaps lessen the stress . . . .").

Kugler is a college teacher, in an exclusively undergraduate biology program. Like other faculty at Radford, he teaches the equivalent of twelve hours per week each semester to anywhere from eighty to one hundred and fifty students. All college teachers reflect on their work, during and after their courses. Kugler is certainly not alone in this. But the image of him in his narrow office, replaying and reassessing the teaching of a particular course, is a good one with which to particularize the academic work of Radford University. He is a good teacher to watch.

In March of 1981, his second year at Radford, he attended a small meeting of faculty called to discuss student writing in the university. In the discussion that followed, he proposed, gingerly, that the teaching of writing should be the responsibility of all faculty. When the suggestion was first made that writing groups be formed among faculty, he joined one and brought to it the drafts of a lab manual he was writing for freshman biology. Kugler made one of the first faculty panel discussion presentations, and he agreed to write it up for publication to the faculty in the first volume of *Working Papers on Writing and Learning*. The first time a group of Radford faculty traveled off-campus to a conference on writing (the 1983 University of Chicago conference on writing and higher order reasoning), Kugler was one of the group. So impressed was he by one of the speakers at that conference—Lucy Cromwell from Alverno College—that he signed up for a special two-year program designed by Alverno to examine the "critical thinking" demands of undergraduate college courses.

Sometimes, he has felt so pressed by other obligations that he has said no. When invited in 1986 to join a group of faculty to examine the shape and direction of Radford's Writing Across the Curriculum program, he declined. He later requested that he not be asked to be a program coordinator, and he has never signed up to teach an "official" writing-intensive course. He speaks now of these decisions with some regret and regards his own participation in the program as very limited. But its influence on his work is unmistakable.

Kugler attended the first Pipestem faculty workshop in 1984 and found it so valuable that he decided to arrange one especially for colleagues in his department. He wanted to create for them an opportunity to have something of the same experience he had had both at Pipestem and in his summer workshops at Alverno College. Though his colleagues might balk at "writing across the curriculum," he said, they would embrace "critical thinking." So, under a different name, he undertook in his own department the faculty-development project Writing Across the Curriculum was conducting for the faculty at large. His "critical thinking" workshop was so successful that the biology department went on to plan and conduct a state-wide conference on critical thinking for high-school biology teachers. Meanwhile, he continued to participate in Writing Across the Curriculum activities, organizing a student-faculty panel discussion on revision and writing a newsletter article on science writing. And he continued to talk informally with his colleagues, urging new members of the biology faculty to familiarize themselves with the program and to join its work. (One of those new colleagues, Sam Zeakes, took

Kugler's advice to heart and has since become one of the program's coordinators.)

All the while, on his "research" desk, Kugler has been preparing a revision of the ant genus *Rogeria*, supported by a grant from the National Science Foundation. That work has prompted him to undertake a study of the comparative anatomy of the sting apparatus in the genus *Gnamptogenys*. His work with Writing Across the Curriculum and critical thinking have led him to develop a new NSF project to revise the curriculum of freshman biology. With another colleague, philosopher of science Joel Hagen, Kugler is working to construct a course that embodies in its very tissue the ideas about teaching and learning that have preoccupied him for ten years.

No one faculty member can epitomize an academic culture, but teachers like Kugler—and folklorist Grace Edwards and geographer Steve Pontius—are the teachers Radford University tries to support and reward. It is in such a context that the history of Writing Across the Curriculum at Radford must be understood. The program's structure and features are legible only against a highly detailed background of purpose and value, for an account of the Writing Across the Curriculum program here necessarily entails a description of the culture of the university.

One strand of that culture is the story of Radford's transformation over the last two decades. Though nearly half the present faculty were not at Radford even ten years ago, the transformation story is sustained by institutional memory. It begins with the arrival of Donald Dedmon as its new president in 1972. He relaxed the social rules on campus, opened the college to male students, increased enrollments, boosted faculty morale by introducing a new participatory system of internal governance, and established a non-profit university foundation to attract private financial assistance. By 1979, Radford College had become Radford University. The story of this change in name, and status, is part of the institutional saga.

Dedmon tells it himself: "I remember walking in one day and announcing to a bewildered, indeed shocked, staff that what this place needed was a name change—immediately. I was too dumb to know how complicated changing the name of an academic institution is." But this phrase of characteristic self-deprecation is followed immediately by pride: "The campaign of this institution to get its name changed was one of the best pieces of collective work (faculty, staff, students, alums and all the others) I've ever seen. Only one person voted against it in any committee or chamber in Richmond. I like to believe that he pressed the wrong button."

Radford's story about itself is a highly selective one. All such stories are. Certain facts, particular episodes, individual personalities collect themselves in a narrative that embodies at least some of the institution's sense of itself. In this case, the transformation story is told most often by the president and by the university's public relations office, lending credit to the criticism that, because it highlights the president's own role, it is self-serving. But it is a larger story than his alone, and its telling certainly serves the institution's purposes. It gives historical resonance to the university's present slogan—"A Spirit of Change"—and it lends connotations to the word "change" of the vigor and freshness of past success.

Yet, for all that, the very vitality of Radford University entails two related uncertainties. First, if it defines itself as embodying the spirit of change—of being willing to take risks, of prizing innovation, of wanting to act quickly and decisively—then the question is: to *what* does it want to change? Second, if it tries to demonstrate its vitality in conspicuous ways—in its physical plant, in its developing athletic programs and artistic offerings, and in the social and cultural life it offers to students—what is its sense of itself in the less conspicuous realms of the mind, of discourse and inquiry? The answers to these questions are not yet clear. But if Radford's academic culture has been uncertain, it is just this uncertainty that has made Writing Across the Curriculum so valuable to it.

The ideas of writing across the curriculum were making their first way into American higher education at just the time when they could serve Radford's particular purposes. The administration sensed considerable potential value for the institution in a writing-across-the-curriculum program. That is why they supported it so assiduously. The faculty who first proposed the program and participated in it felt its value for themselves as teachers, and the more energetically they worked, the richer and more satisfying its felt benefits became. It is likely that neither the faculty nor the administration realized how these different values would mutually reinforce each other, but their dynamic interaction has been from the start a central fact of the program's life.

In the professional literature about writing across the curriculum, the most pressing recent question is how to make it last. The current consensus seems to be that the best way to ensure its survival is to make it part of the administrative structure of the institution. That way, as Susan McLeod says, it will be "part of the established order" (*College Composition and Communication 40 [1989]: 342*). Toby Fulwiler and Art Young agree: "Institutions must develop a more or less permanent structure whereby writing-across-the-curriculum advocacy is ever renewed and expanded" *(Programs That Work,* 294). In "Writing Across the Curriculum and the Communications Movement: Some Lessons from the Past," David Russell draws the same conclusion. "The fundamental problem of WAC," Russell writes, "is not so much pedagogical as political, not how to create a sound program (that has been possible for decades), but rather how to administer it, how to place it firmly in the complex organizational structure of the university" (*College Composition and Communication* 38 [1987]: 191).

The faculty who have worked most closely with Radford's Writing Across the Curriculum program have been of mixed minds about its politics, but they have been strongly committed to its pedagogy. Perhaps their emphasis on community, dialogue, and pedagogy will prove to have been a mistake. But they have felt that using writing to bring faculty together in a campus-wide discussion of teaching and learning should be their first concern. Such an approach seems to fit the character of the institution in which they teach. The program is personal, informal, ad hoc. It depends on the energy and commitment of individuals. It minimizes both bureaucracy and orthodoxy. It embodies the university's claim that the "teaching transaction" is in fact its primary reason for being.

But will it last? No one knows. In an institution where innovation is prized, will it change? Probably, but it is impossible to say how. Will its name become anachronistic? In important ways, it already has. The story of Writing Across the Curriculum is in one sense the story of its name developing, changing, acquiring new meaning in the context of a particular university culture. And it is the story of individuals.

"Symbiosis," Chuck Kugler says. "That's a good analogy for it. Never mind the connotations of 'parasite.' The thing about symbiosis is that both organisms benefit. Real benefits. The relation only works because each gives the other things they really need for life. That's what happened here," he says. "The story of Radford and Writing Across the Curriculum is a story of symbiosis."

Later this summer, Kugler will be on his way to an international symposium to read a paper discussing *Gnamptogenys* stings. But right now he has to finish these notes about his evolution course. On his research desk, his specimens and his drawings are waiting. He turns back from his visitor to the computer screen, rereads, and then begins again to write.